WINNING TABLE TENNIS

Dan Seemiller
5-time U.S. Singles Champion, 11-time U.S. Doubles Champion
16-year member U.S. Team, International Coach

Mark Holowchak
University of Pittsburgh

Human Kinetics

Library of Congress Cataloging-in-Publication Data

Seemiller, Dan, 1954-
   Winning table tennis : skills, drills, and strategies / Dan
Seemiller, Mark Holowchak.
      p.   cm.
   Includes index.
   ISBN 0-88011-520-3
   1. Table tennis.   I. Holowchak, Mark, 1958-   . II. Title.
GV1005.S46   1997   96-8102
796.34'6--dc20   CIP
ISBN: 0-88011-520-3

Developmental Editor: Nanette Smith; **Assistant Editor:** Henry Woolsey; **Editorial Assistant:** Coree Schutter; **Copyeditor:** Denelle Eknes; **Proofreader:** Jacqueline Seebaum; **Indexer:** Joan Griffits; **Graphic Designer:** Judy Henderson; **Graphic Artist:** Ruby Zimmerman; **Photo Editor:** Boyd LaFoon; **Cover Designer:** Jack Davis; **Photographer (cover):** Terry Wilde Studio; **Photographers (interior):** Terry Wilde, John Oros; **Illustrators:** Studio 2-D, Tim Offenstein; **Printer:** United Graphics

Human Kinetics books are available at special discounts for bulk purchase. Special editions or book excerpts can also be created to specification. For details, contact the Special Sales Manager at Human Kinetics.

Printed in the United States of America   10 9 8 7 6 5 4 3 2 1
Human Kinetics
Web site: http://www.humankinetics.com/

United States: Human Kinetics, P.O. Box 5076, Champaign, IL 61825-5076
1-800-747-4457
e-mail: humank@hkusa.com

Canada: Human Kinetics, Box 24040, Windsor, ON N8Y 4Y9
1-800-465-7301 (in Canada only)
e-mail: humank@hkcanada.com

Europe: Human Kinetics, P.O. Box IW14, Leeds LS16 6TR, United Kingdom
(44) 1132 781708
e-mail: humank@hkeurope.com

Australia: Human Kinetics, 57A Price Avenue, Lower Mitcham, South Australia 5062
(08) 277 1555
e-mail: humank@hkaustralia.com

New Zealand: Human Kinetics, P.O. Box 105-231, Auckland 1
(09) 523 3462
e-mail: humank@hknewz.com

Contents

Foreword

Winning Table Tennis comes from a winner, author Danny Seemiller, and that's just one reason for you to read it. Among Seemiller's many accomplishments, he is a USA Table Tennis Hall of Famer and five-time U.S. National Men's Singles Champion.

This is the most serious, no-nonsense book on table tennis that I've read in 40 years of playing and reading about the sport. I'm a retired 65-year-old, and I belong to an association whose 80-year-old members still play fierce tournaments regularly; I found plenty to learn in these pages, and I expect to put it all to good use.

Danny became a world-class player by *living* table tennis, and his work ethic permeates every page of this book. Young or old, if you want to win at tournament table tennis, you have to work at it. You must be as athletic as possible: to have watched Seemiller play is to have seen a well-conditioned athlete. Not surprisingly, he emphasizes the components of physical fitness and tells you how to achieve it, giving suggestions on everything from diet to appropriate shoes.

The writing itself speaks to his attitude: This is a lean book, without padding or fat, coauthored by the knowledgeable Mark Holowchak. You'll learn exactly what anaerobic conditioning, aerobic training, and experience to undertake for competition.

After eight world championships, Danny has seen and analyzed (and often beaten) every type of player. Taking advantage of that experience, he explains a variety of tactics you can use in competition. He knows that as intense as your playing must be, you also must give your mind and body recovery time. He explains how to time your peak performances to correlate with your long-term goals.

Danny likes to talk about his "thinking man's style," and he makes the case here for learning to focus both before and during competition. In *Winning Table Tennis* he also gives solid tips to best utilize your senses and gems of advice on techniques and strategies.

My sons, Scott and Eric, who are U.S. Men's Singles champions, owe much of their success to attending Seemiller training camps over the years and to benefiting from Danny's unselfish sharing of his experience. The Seemillers (Danny and Ricky) and the Boggans—what savage matches these teammates and friends have had—and what good times. At numerous tournaments, I rooted passionately for my boys against Danny, and he never took offense. Danny is now the U.S. Over-40 Men's Singles and Doubles champion. Between all the lines in *Winning Table Tennis* you'll sense his love for the sport. As I recommend this book so highly to you, I feel certain you'll agree that any aspiring player is sure to enjoy the game more after taking its advice to heart. After all, this book teaches you how to win—and winning, as we all know, is great fun!

Tim Boggan
ITTF Vice President
Three-Time USATT Past President

*A*cknowledgments

I would like to thank several key people who were instrumental to my success as a table tennis player.

My family, especially my two brothers, Rick and Randy, who were always there when I needed practice. To my two coaches, Dell Sweeris and Houshang Bozorgzadeh, who taught me that hard work never goes unrewarded. Also to the Tamasu Company, makers of Butterfly table tennis equipment and their American distributor, Martin-Kilpatrick Table Tennis Co. of North Carolina. Without their sponsorship and support I never could have continued playing this sport all these years.

I'd also like to acknowledge Mr. Mark Holowchak, the co-author, who helped push me to do this project. His insight and knowledge of sport psychology added considerably to this book.

Preface

Our collaboration is chiefly an effort to provide table-tennis enthusiasts with a guidebook for achieving excellence in this sport. We're assuming you have some familiarity with the fundamentals of the game so we focus on providing you with useful and current information on how you can become a better, more knowledgeable competitor. We talk about both the physical and mental aspects of table-tennis preparation and play, as well as supplemental factors like nutrition, sleep, conditioning, and workout recovery. The book's comprehensiveness and topicality make it, we feel, necessary for all aspiring table-tennis players and useful for serious athletes in other sports as well.

What makes our book unique is that it draws from the experience of arguably the finest American table-tennis player, Dan Seemiller (5 times U.S. Singles Champion; 11 times U.S. Doubles Champion; U.S. team member from 1972-1985 and 1991-1993; once ranked 19th in the world; U.S.A. National Men's Coach from 1988-1990; and president of the United States Table Tennis Association from 1990 to 1995), and from current sport research in psychological, physiological, nutritional, and medical journals and books. It is our hope that this blend will afford you a fresh and sober approach to the game, whether you are a beginner or a table-tennis fanatic.

Part I

SHARPENING YOUR SKILLS

Currently the world's highest ranked player, Wang Tao gets full extension on this backhand smash.

Chapter *1*

Standard Strokes and Advanced Variations

One of the top-ranked players in the United States, David Zhuang blocks back a strong loop.

*I*n this chapter we focus on the most fundamental strokes of the game. As a serious player, you should be capable of performing each of these strokes well, even if some of them will not figure significantly in your style of play. In addition to the fundamental strokes, we give an account of variations that may be of service to advanced-level players and professionals. Before we begin stroking, let us say a few words about gripping the paddle.

THE GRIP

Among the best players of table tennis, there are a few grips of choice. These are the shakehands grip, the penhold grip, and the Seemiller grip. In what follows, we describe each grip and discuss its advantages and disadvantages.

The Shakehands Grip

This is the preferred grip of most players in the world, and it is becoming even more popular with the ascendancy of European players in the world rankings in recent years. You perform the grip by grasping the bat as if shaking hands with the handle. Rest your pointing finger across the bottom of one side of the blade. The bottom three fingers grip the handle and your thumb rests along the lower part of the other side of the blade (see figures 1.1 and 1.2).

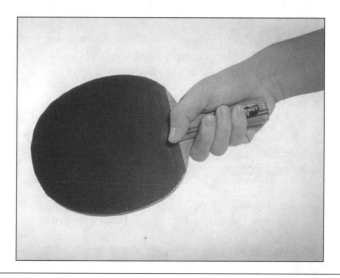

Figure 1.1 Shakehands grip.

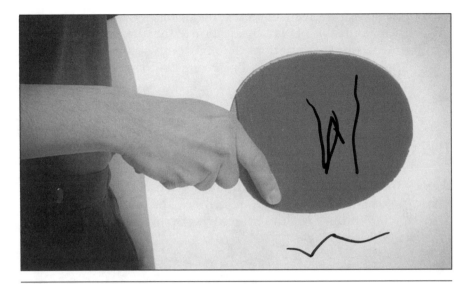

Figure 1.2 Shakehands grip, alternate view.

Of the grips we mention, this is the most versatile, allowing both a strong forehand and backhand. With the shakehands grip, you have freedom of wrist. You can keep your wrist loose to increase the spin on a particular shot or you may stiffen it for a higher percentage, lower spin shot. For a strong, sure backhand, grip the bat snugly and at the top of the handle. To vary the spin on forehand and backhand shots, move your grip up or down the handle: up for less spin and less wrist flexibility, down for greater spin and more wrist flexibility. The 1995-1996 and 1993-1994 world champions, Kong Linghui (China) and Jean-Philippe Gatien (France), and the 1992 Olympic gold-medal winner, Jan Ove Waldner (Sweden), use this grip.

Chinese Penhold Grip

The Chinese penhold grip is similar to holding a pen between the thumb and forefinger (see figures 1.3 and 1.4). Your racket head points downward, with your other three fingers curled and centered onto the back of the racket, while the bat handle, held between the thumb and forefinger, points upward. Because your wrist is relatively free, this is an excellent grip for both forehand stroking and forehand serving.

The main drawback of this grip is that, utilizing the same side of the blade for the backhand, it cramps the backhand and makes a

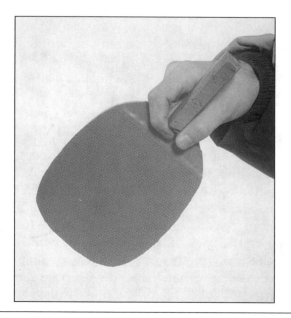

Figure 1.3   Chinese penhold grip.

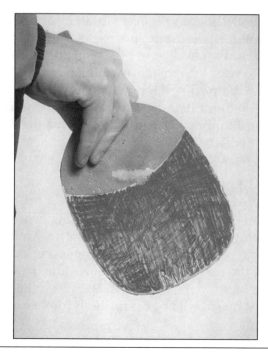

Figure 1.4   Chinese penhold grip, alternate view.

forceful shot from this side of the table almost impossible. Consequently, most players with this grip play their forehand 75 percent of the time. Because it requires exceptional footwork, it is not good for older players or those who are slow-of-foot. The 1995-1996 world-champion runner-up, Liu Guoliang of China, uses this grip.

Japanese and Korean Penhold Grip

This grip is similar to the Chinese penhold grip except that you do not hold the bat straight up and down, but directly out to the side. Here the bat, nestled tightly between the thumb and forefinger, becomes nearly an extension of your arm (see figure 1.5). Unlike the Chinese penhold grip, your other three fingers are fully extended and centered down the back of the blade. Because the bat is nearly an extension of the arm with this grip, it allows for a powerful, crisp forehand and an easier backhand than the Chinese grip. However, with the wrist mostly locked into position, touch and spin shots are more difficult. As with the Chinese grip, because the backhand is still weak here, good footwork is essential. Lu Lin (China), 1995-1996 world doubles champion, Kim Taek Soo (Korea), the 1992 Olympic bronze medalist, and Yoo Nam Kyu (Korea), the 1988 Olympic gold medalist, are world-ranked players who use this grip.

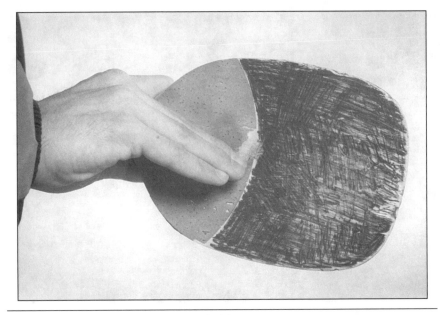

Figure 1.5 Japanese and Korean penhold grip.

Seemiller Grip

As pictured in figures 1.6 and 1.7, the Seemiller grip is somewhat of a basement technique, a grip that combines elements of the shakehands and penhold grips. To use this grip, hold the paddle in a shakehands fashion but with a quarter turn so the thumb and forefinger grip the sides of the bat. As you will notice, here and throughout the book, Danny is a lefty. Keep that in mind in the photos of Danny's technique.

In all, the Seemiller grip allows great wrist action on the forehand and, consequently, a powerful forehand shot. However, similar to the penhold grips, when playing a backhand you utilize the same side of the blade as the forehand and are limited by your lack of wrist action. Nevertheless, this is a fine grip for backhand blocking.

You should cover the "unused" side of the blade with an off-rubber like antispin, and you may switch it to the playing side in the middle of a rally to confound your opponent. By switching sides of the bat and manipulating the grip, you can make two to three major technique changes during rallies. Different types of rubber often used with this style will make return of service easier for you (because return of service with an off-rubber is not as difficult) and even more challenging for opponents (because they may not know which side

Figure 1.6   Seemiller grip.

Figure 1.7   Seemiller grip, alternate view.

of the racket you are using). The 1983 rule change that the different colors of rubber must be used on each side of the racket has severely limited the advantages of this grip. Like the penhold grips, the Seemiller grip is falling increasingly into disuse.

THE STROKES

In the description of the strokes that follows, we illustrate proper technique for right-handed players only. Left-handed players need only reverse the description. We follow this convention throughout the book.

The Forehand Counterdrive

The forehand counterdrive is one of the basic strokes of the game (see figures 1.8, 1.9, and 1.10). Advanced players can sustain rallies of 50 or more counterdrives without missing. Generally, the stroke looks like a partial salute, with a slight pivot at both the midsection

Figure 1.8   Forehand counterdrive, part one.

Figure 1.9   Forehand counterdrive, part two.

Figure 1.10 Forehand counterdrive, part three.

and the shoulders toward the center of the table. At the beginning, your forearm should lead the stroke—that is, it should be the first thing to cross the frontal plane of your body. Throughout the stroke, keep your swinging elbow at least three inches away from your body and your wrist stiff. With a stable wrist, your bat should almost be an extension of your forearm.

Concerning ball contact, always aim to strike the ball at the top of the bounce (unless you desire a quicker shot, in which case you should contact the ball just before the top of the bounce). By striking the ball at the top of the bounce, you will have more time to make sure of a sound stroke. The sound at contact should be solid and crisp, not "spinny."

Begin the shot with your racket above the waist. As your arm moves through the ball, never let it cross your body at follow-through so it ends up at your left shoulder. At follow-through, always keep your racket on the same side of your body as the bat hand—that is, right-handed players should end their counters on the right side of their body; left-handers on their left. A lengthy follow-through will not allow you sufficient time to ready yourself for a proper return. Therefore, complete the forehand counter at about eye level.

Your legs and trunk play only a minor role throughout this stroke. Keep your feet slightly farther than shoulder-width apart and your left leg a little in front of the right. Your left foot should be perpendicular to the table, while the right foot points slightly outward. As the stroke begins, shift your weight from the right leg to the left one at contact. Throughout the stroke, your free arm moves with your shoulders to improve balance, in opposition to your swinging arm.

Keep your forehand hitting zone (zone in which you should make contact) entirely within your body. As figure 1.11a shows, player X is roughly parallel to the end of the table (i.e., facing it squarely) and must contact the ball at the front of his body, at point C_1, if he wishes to go crosscourt. For a shot down the line, he must open himself to a position of nearly two o'clock with respect to the table and make contact at the rear of his body, at point C_3 (figure 1.11c). To hit to the center of the table, he must contact the ball near the middle of his body, at C_2 (figure 1.11b). Here he is positioned between the crosscourt and down-the-line shots, at about one o'clock with respect to the table's end. These shifts in foot placement and contact points when going crosscourt, toward the middle, or down the line apply to all other forehand strokes.

The Forehand Smash

This is the most fundamental and effective put-away stroke of the game. Regardless of your style of play, you must be able to execute this shot against a variety of spins if you wish to compete successfully as a tournament player or professional.

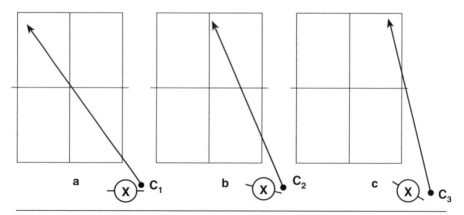

Figure 1.11 Forehand counter and forehand hitting zone. Note how the contact point, C, is entirely within *X*'s body for each of the three placements.

Against Topspin. Mechanically, this stroke is similar to the forehand counterdrive. The forehand smash against topspin differs, however, in that the motion of your swing is longer, your racket speed is faster, your weight shift is quicker and more powerful, and the blade is a bit more closed (see figures 1.12, 1.13, and 1.14). Standing relatively straight at the beginning of the stroke, move your right foot back, pointed parallel to the table's end and perpendicular to your left foot. Then, swinging your free arm backward, shift your weight forward and drive through the ball powerfully and surely. Smash the ball at the top of the bounce and off the front foot. Your arm, above the ball, should strike slightly down on the ball and you should keep your racket face closed throughout the stroke. In this manner, the plane of your swing, from beginning to end, is downward.

When smashing, it is always preferable to go crosscourt, because you have more table to work with and you are less likely to miss. On balls that land short, you may choose to smash into your opponent's body or down the line for greater effect. On such shots, your swing will be slower and shorter because, hanging over the table, you cannot get the same shoulder rotation you would have if you hit crosscourt. Therefore, your swing is mostly with the arm.

Figure 1.12 Forehand smash against topspin, part one.

Figure 1.13   Forehand smash against topspin, part two.

Figure 1.14   Forehand smash against topspin, part three.

Against Underspin.   When hitting against underspin, because a ball with underspin stays closer to the net after it hits your end of the table than one with topspin, move closer to the table. Begin your swing from just above the top of the table and, with an opened blade, drive your racket upward a little. Make contact off the back foot and follow through in a full-salute motion, approximately to the top of the head.

Because this ball usually bounces short on the table, you may often find yourself too far back from the ball when you begin your swing. Consequently, you will be unable to follow through properly and the ball will likely go into the net. Get as close to the table as you need (often you will have to place your front foot under the table) and contact the ball as close to your rear foot as possible.

There are several common mistakes players make concerning the kill. First, players often anxiously jump at the ball. When you jump toward a ball moving toward you, it becomes difficult to catch the ball at the top of the bounce. Be patient here, wait for the ball to come to you, then put it away. Second, players often strike the ball outside the body—that is, outside the proper contact zone. Your striking position must be within the body, not out in front of it (a very common mistake) or behind it. Failure to strike the ball within your body results in a loss of control and, frequently, a smash that misses the table. A third mistake is that players too often begin the stroke from the crouch instead of the upright position. By crouching, you combine useless upward motion with the legs with the required forward motion. When smashing against topspin, you need no upward motion. Direct all of your force forward and slightly downward. Greater forward motion will increase the speed of your bat at contact, thereby increasing the speed of the ball off your bat and the effectiveness of your kill. Come out of your crouch before you begin

---

Key Points

1. Wait for the ball to come to you and catch it at the top of the bounce before putting it away.
2. Strike the ball from within the forehand contact zone (i.e., from entirely within your body).
3. When smashing against topspin, stand nearly erect and direct all your force forward.
4. Practice this shot as you do all others.

your swing. Last, players too often assume that if they have no problem with their forehand counter, they have no problem with their forehand kill. Being a put-away shot, the timing differs from all other shots. You must practice smashing to get your timing down and be good at this shot.

The Backhand Counterdrive

Like the forehand counterdrive, you must learn the backhand counter before you can hope to play competitively. Crouched and with knees bent, begin with the front of your body nearly parallel to the end of the table. With the blade of your bat slightly opened and just left of center to your body, take a short backswing from directly behind the ball. Follow through after contact, straightening your arm for power and breaking your wrist for topspin. (The wrist is *very* active throughout this stroke.) Move up on your toes during the shot and point your bat toward the targeted area. By moving up on your toes at contact, the backhand counterdrive is a much less balanced stroke than the forehand counterdrive, but the shortness of the stroke will allow you plenty of time to ready yourself for the next shot (see figures 1.15, 1.16, and 1.17.)

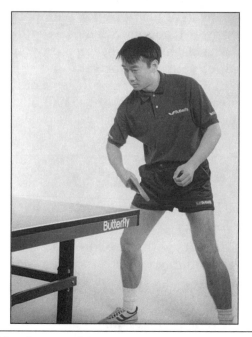

Figure 1.15 Backhand counterdrive, part one.

Figure 1.16   Backhand counterdrive, part two.

Figure 1.17   Backhand counterdrive, part three.

Unlike the forehand, the backhand hitting zone is very small. For this reason, position yourself before the shot at the hitting zone so you do not have to reach out to the ball at contact. As figure 1.18a illustrates, X contacts the ball slightly out in front of her body for a crosscourt backhand, at point C_1, with her left foot just out in front of her right. To hit toward the table's center, she must contact the ball at point C_2 while standing parallel to the table (figure 1.18b). To go down the line, she must contact the ball even closer to her body while shifting her feet so her right foot is slightly in front of the left (figure 1.18c). These shifts in contact points and footwork apply equally well to all other backhand shots.

The contact point is usually quick off the bounce, before the ball's high point, but this varies according to the incoming speed of the ball. For fast-moving balls, a contact point just after the bounce is ideal because it facilitates a speedy return. For slower moving balls, strike the ball higher off the bounce, and more forcefully and powerfully. Again, as with all hits, contact must be crisp and sure, with your swinging arm going through the ball. Land the ball deep on your opponent's court with a light topspin. The backhand counter is not a stroke that wins points outright. Use it to sustain volleys and maneuver an opponent so you may set yourself up for a point-winning shot like the forehand smash or forehand loop kill.

You may want to incorporate a harder and more forceful variation of the backhand counterdrive into your repertoire: the backhand "corner-stick." At contact, keep your blade slightly opened and push forward quickly to create greater racket speed than with

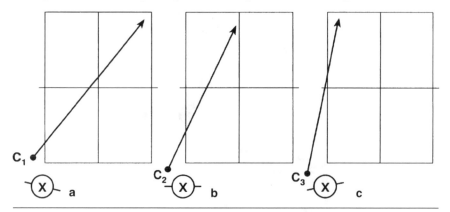

Figure 1.18 Backhand counter and backhand hitting zone. In contrast to the forehand, the backhand hitting zone is outside the body. Here the contact point, C, lies in front of the body and gets closer to it as X shifts from the crosscourt to a down-the-line placement.

the backhand counterdrive. You can use the corner-stick as a variation in a sequence of backhand counterdrives in practice and as a means of gaining the initiative during match play.

The Forehand Loop

In today's power-and-spin game, the forehand loop is perhaps the most effective weapon in your offensive arsenal.

Against Topspin.   The forehand loop against topspin is often mistakenly seen as an uneven mixture of two separate motions: one, motion toward the ball; the other, motion over the ball (see figures 1.19, 1.20, and 1.21). The actual motion of this shot is simply back to front and slightly upward at the follow-through. From the ready position and away from the table, bring the right leg back about one foot behind the left, positioning the right foot so it is nearly perpendicular to the end of the table. Then shift your weight onto the right leg by turning at the waist and shoulders and extending the bat hand backward. As the ball approaches, shift your weight forward as your bat arm drives toward the ball. Contact the top of the ball just after the top of the bounce with a closed racket and a grazing motion. Follow through

Figure 1.19   Forehand loop against topspin, part one.

Figure 1.20   Forehand loop against topspin, part two.

Figure 1.21   Forehand loop against topspin, part three.

with your swinging arm fully extended to the front of your body. At the finish, your right foot moves forward with the momentum of your body, which squares with the table upon completion, while your left foot falls back a little.

Throughout the swing, keep your center of gravity relatively high. Furthermore, always use at least a three-quarter swing, and do not follow through beyond a salute. Too long a follow-through will not allow enough time to prepare for a return. Though we recommend that you make contact just after the top of the bounce, you can perform the topspin loop before, just at, or anytime after the top of the bounce. This makes this shot the most flexible timing shot in the game.

Overall, because the amount of topspin you use is unlikely to trouble your opponent, speed is more important than spin when performing this shot. During practice, build up the speed on consecutive loops, concentrating on utilizing the legs, hips, and waist as well as the shoulders and arms to generate power.

For a change, try either hooking a loop or an inside-out loop. To *hook a loop,* contact the outside top of the ball by bending your wrist downward and following through by circling around the ball. Figures 1.22 and 1.23 show the difference between driving a loop and hooking a loop. By doing so, you will decrease the amount of topspin and make the ball hook left with sidespin at the end of the shot. At the end of the shot, the forehand racket side will be facing you. For an *inside-out loop,* graze the inside-top of the ball with bent wrist,

Figure 1.22   Ilija Lupulesku of Yugoslavia drives a loop.

Figure 1.23   Ilija Lupulesku hooks a loop at the 1995 World Team Cup in Atlanta.

breaking the wrist at contact so the ball will curl to the right. Upon completion of the stroke, in contrast to the hook loop, the forehand racket side will be facing your opponent. Both variations of the topspin loop reduce the amount of topspin and give instead some difficult-to-negotiate sidespin. Attempt such shots only against slow-moving counters and blocks.

Against Underspin.   The forehand loop against underspin, as pictured in figures 1.24, 1.25, and 1.26, differs significantly from the topspin variation. Unlike the loop against topspin, spin is more

Figure 1.24   Forehand loop against underspin, part one.

Figure 1.25 Forehand loop against underspin, part two.

Figure 1.26 Forehand loop against underspin, part three.

important than speed here. Start by positioning yourself close to the table. Drop your right shoulder and bring your racket low to the ground, with the blade slightly opened, by shifting your weight down onto your right leg. The paddle's head should point to the ground. Next, powerfully surge upward, not forward, with your shoulders, arms, and especially your legs. With your free arm starting high, pull it down as your bat arm comes up to the ball. The free arm acts as a counterbalance throughout and is an important key to a successful loop —especially when you are out of position, off balance, or moving.

Make contact one or two inches after the top of the bounce. At contact, lean back a little so you are under the ball, keeping the plane of your swing just behind your right knee. Graze the ball at either the bottom or the back by adjusting the paddle angle, depending on the amount of underspin, and break your wrist. Close the racket more for light underspin (see figure 1.27), open it more for heavy underspin (see figure1.28). For additional topspin or against heavier underspin, break the wrist more forcefully upon contact.

Upon completion, you should leave the ground momentarily, while remaining squared to the table. Against very heavy underspin, you may even find yourself falling backward a little. Follow through with your racket slightly above your head. Overall, this loop should be powerful, not timid.

If you have not properly mastered this shot, first develop the swing. Concentrate on a mechanically correct and strong swing whether or not you can consistently hit the ball on the table. Once your swing becomes mechanically correct, consistency will follow. Patience and persistence are keys here because the shot requires great strength, skill, and precise timing. You may have to work up to a certain level of conditioning before being able to effectively utilize this shot in game-situation conditions.

Three Variations.   There are three types of loop that you can use against underspin. At one extreme, especially against very heavy underspin, this is a slow, high-arced spin loop. This stroke is perpendicular to the ground from start to finish, and the goal is to set yourself up for a more aggressive shot, like a loop kill or smash. Open your racket in proportion to the quantity of underspin. At the other extreme, against lighter underspin, you may utilize a fast, forward-driving loop. Catch the ball just after the top of the bounce with a slightly less-opened bat and try not to graze the ball. Here, by rotating the hips and shoulders toward the table, this loop generates

Figure 1.27   Paddle position for forehand loop against light underspin.

Figure 1.28   Paddle position for forehand loop against heavy underspin.

considerable forward thrust. Your aim is to win the point outright. A third loop against underspin is one that combines elements of both. It is aggressive, yet conservative. The grazing, the upward motion, and the bat angle all should be less than that of the arced loop, but more than that of the drive loop. The contact point should not be as high as that of the drive loop, but not as low as that of the spin loop.

Key Points

Some common mistakes in this important shot are the following:

1. Contacting the ball too far in front of your body
2. Not dropping the bat low enough before contact
3. Catching the ball outside the power zone

The Backhand Loop

Though not more difficult to perform and not as versatile and effective as the forehand loop, the backhand loop is a definite asset to offensive players, especially those who are less swift of foot or who prefer a more balanced attack.

Against Topspin. Unlike the forehand loop, for the backhand loop against topspin, do not bend the knees so much during this shot. Positioning yourself at least two feet from the table, begin this loop from a slight squatlike position, keeping your racket head down at the start. Thrust upward with your legs while swinging both upward and forward. Graze the ball by hitting its top. Because there is minimal rotation at the hips and midsection with this loop, your shoulders, forearm, and wrist will generate most of the force and bat speed (see figures 1.29, 1.30, and 1.31).

Against Underspin. Against underspin, begin from a full-squat position. Open the paddle and fully extend your swinging arm so the racket points downward. Drive upward with your legs and graze the ball by hitting its bottom with a stroke that is perpendicular to the ground. Concentrate on snapping your wrist at contact to ensure adequate lift and spin (see figures 1.32, 1.33, and 1.34).

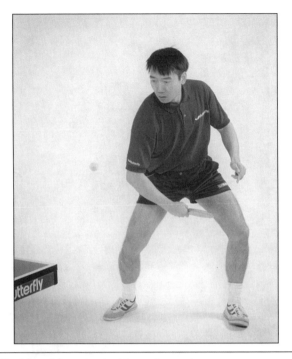

Figure 1.29 Backhand loop against topspin, part one.

Figure 1.30 Backhand loop against topspin, part two.

Figure 1.31   Backhand loop against topspin, part three.

Figure 1.32   Backhand loop against underspin, part one.

Figure 1.33   Backhand loop against underspin, part two.

Figure 1.34   Backhand loop against underspin, part three.

The Lob

The lob is exclusively a defensive shot. It is performed many feet away from the table against a smash or a forcefully driven loop, used often when players are caught out of position or off balance. It is an attempt to get back into the point and should never be a strategy to defeat an opponent. Because lobbing will always put you at a disadvantage, use it with discretion or only in desperate situations. Mechanically, the lob is similar to the arced loop. Like the arced loop, arc and good topspin are the two critical factors.

Forehand Lob.   To execute a forehand lob, work yourself during a few forehand counters to a position at least eight feet away from the table. Crouch with your right leg slightly behind the left. Beginning with your bat lower than the ball, strike the ball with a grazing motion approximately at waist level. Follow through with your arm fully extended over the top of your head.

Backhand Lob.   For the backhand, crouch behind the ball as it comes, and graze it at about waist level. Again, follow through fully. Adjust speed, spin, and height for effect. Always try to land your lobs deep on the table with ample topspin to ensure that your opponent has less table with which to work.

The Block

The block is a defensive-posture shot made against heavily spun topspin shots or smashes. Players seldom block to win a point outright. They block to keep the ball in play or to set up a point-winning shot. Blocking requires good balance and much finesse. When blocking using the shakehands grip, keep the bat to the side at contact for a forehand, but directly in front of the body for a backhand.

Against a Loop.   When blocking against a loop, block from the top of or above the ball, while on your toes, and press down with your bat arm at contact. When blocking a loop made against your own underspin, block the ball right off the bounce. When blocking a loop made against topspin, wait a little longer and cover the ball at impact. For either variation, to effect a quicker return, block on top of the ball and push forward. This will act much the same as a counter, using an opponent's spin to your advantage (see figures 1.35 and 1.36).

Figure 1.35 Backhand block.

Figure 1.36 Forehand block.

Against a Smash.   While up at the table and attempting to block against a smash, open your blade and cushion the ball back to your opponent's end by relaxing your grip. Here, it is best for you to try to play yourself back into the point instead of trying to win it. Consequently, a well-placed block is usually the best option. To have any chance of trying to place the block, however, you need to remain balanced. Often, this is asking too much; just returning the ball and not losing the point outright is frequently the best you can do against a smash. If you are up at the table, any return will be a good one, for your opponent will have very little time to get ready for another smash.

Some elite players, like J. O. Waldner and the author (Danny Seemiller), use sidespin blocks to make it even more difficult for an opponent to attack. For instance, on his backhand against a loop, Waldner sometimes cuts across the left top of the ball with a slight forward jab. This makes his opponent's next loop more difficult, because the sidespin keeps the ball closer to the net and draws his opponent in from a deeper position.

The Underspin Push

The push is a neutral-position underspin shot, done in front of the body. Do not push to win points, but use the push to jockey for position. Move quickly to the ball and begin the stroke with the racket at the same height as the ball. Strike the ball on its bottom quickly off the bounce, aiming either for a short drop just over the net, a middle drop (which is the safest but least effective), or a deep drop near the end line. Contacting the ball quickly off the bounce gives your opponent less time to react to the shot.

Forehand Push.   On the forehand side, step the right foot up to the table and, keeping your head down and blade open, cut through the ball with one fluid motion. Never begin with a closed blade, then open the blade by curling under the ball with the wrist at contact. Follow through in a straight line, then move back to the ready position (see figures 1.37 and 1.38).

Backhand Push.   On the backhand side, keep your head low and, beginning with the blade in front of the body, cut through the ball with the forearm and wrist. Again, it is essential that you stroke through the ball to create underspin and not just angle it back using your opponent's spin. Angling the ball back is risky and difficult,

Figure 1.37 Forehand push, part one.

Figure 1.38 Forehand push, part two.

and any misread of the spin on the ball will result in a return in the net or over the table. (see figures 1.39 and 1.40).

Drop Shot.   The short push or "drop" shot is a variation of the push used especially against underspin balls that bounce close to your side of the net. To execute the drop shot, just like the push, catch the ball quickly off the bounce. With your racket underneath the ball, stroke the ball lightly, using little wrist, and, unlike the push, do *not* follow through. The key to a successful drop shot is keeping your shot very close to the net on your opponent's side of the table. Rarely use this shot against medium or long underspin.

The Chop

The chop is a defensive stroke, used by players who would rather frustrate or wear down their opponents than overpower them. Through chopping, a defensive player can impart varying degrees of underspin to different places on the table. The chop differs from the push in that, first, you make contact on the descent instead of the ascent of the ball and, second, you use a much fuller motion and many major muscle groups.

Figure 1.39   Backhand push, part one.

Figure 1.40 Backhand push, part two.

Forehand Chop. For the forehand, start away from the table, in a crouched stance with the right leg trailing the left. With the racket blade open and the bat arm bent and held about head high, cut down toward the ball, striking beneath the ball and following through by extending the arm fully downward and somewhat forward (see figures 1.41 and 1.42).

Backhand Chop. When chopping from the backhand side, while in a crouch stance with the left leg trailing the right, cut down and beneath the ball and follow through fully by extending your arm downward. At impact, break your wrist for additional spin (see figures 1.43 and 1.44).

For both types of chop, vary the spin for diversity by varying the amount of wrist employed.

The Wrist Flick

Use the wrist flick chiefly against short underspin or no-spin serves and shots. Against underspin, step in with your right foot (whether forehand or backhand), lay your wrist open while just under the ball, and flick up and over the ball. Against no spin, close your bat more before contact so it is perpendicular to the table and flick your wrist over the ball from behind it (see figures 1.45 and 1.46).

Figure 1.41 Forehand chop, part one.

Figure 1.42 Forehand chop, part two.

Figure 1.43 Backhand chop, part one.

Figure 1.44 Backhand chop, part two.

This shot, though riskier than the push, allows variety in your shot making and, if done effectively, can initiate a potent attack off a short serve or drop shot.

Figure 1.45   Wrist flick, part one.

Figure 1.46   Wrist flick, part two.

Chapter 2

Serves and Return of Serves

Korea's Kim Taek Soo readies himself for an aggressive return of service.

Serves and return of serves are the most neglected aspects of serious table-tennis play. Practice of these is usually something

players do when, after a thorough training session, they are fully exhausted and have a few minutes to waste or when an important tournament is a few days away. Both approaches are misguided. Service and service return are just as important to table tennis as pitching and hitting are to baseball. Imagine a baseball team practicing certain offensive and defensive skills, such as running and fielding, all during spring training, but not working on its pitching or hitting until just a few days before opening day. The results would be catastrophic. Yet this is what table-tennis players do all the time when they do not devote enough time to serving and returning serves before competition.

SERVES

Good table-tennis serves do more than merely put the ball into play. If you have strong serves, you will consistently be able to initiate the attack and control the flow of play, leaving your opponents off balance and scoring some outright winners. Often, by having good serves, you can beat opponents with smoother, more mechanically sound strokes and lesser serves. Because of its importance, you should spend a minimum of 25 percent of your practice time serving (and returning serves).

Working on your serves is the fastest and easiest way to improve your game. This aspect of the game is more technical than physical. Constant practice pays dividends for all types of players, regardless of their physical conditioning. The server has a decided advantage, and service aggressiveness, through planned third-ball attack, enables you to capitalize on this edge.

For effective serves, your service motion is important and the speed, spin, and placement of the ball are also critical. Service motion is the rhythm of your serve: ball toss, weight exchange, and contact point. In addition, serves are highly complex and the best servers vary their spin, speed, and placement of the ball deceptively. Often, from the same look, for example, the receiver may get a short topspin-sidespin serve, a short underspin-sidespin serve, or a long and fast serve with topspin or no spin. Moreover, good servers generally use varied grips to impart the different speeds and spins, and wrist action is a vital part of this.

Net clearance is also significant. When serving, keep your body low at contact by crouching with your legs. Contact the ball as close to the top of the table as possible and push down with your legs to ensure a low trajectory over the net.

It is important to have and utilize serves that set up point-winning shots. Like all other players, you have a favorite or best shot. Consequently, you should serve so you are in a position to use this shot by the third or the fifth ball. For instance, if you are a looper, short side-underspin, straight-underspin, or no-spin serves are best. If you are a counterdrive player, side-topspin or straight-topspin serves will benefit you. Choppers or blockers may prefer long and spinny serves. Before play, consider which type of service is most effective against a certain opponent. If you are serious about winning, match play is not the time for experimentation.

For all serves and variations of them, you have to be able to place the ball short and long as well as down the line and crosscourt for greatest benefit. For an effective short serve, land the ball on your end of the table about six inches from the end line so the ball strikes the receiver's innermost one-third of the court, nearest the net (zones 7, 8, and 9 of figure 2.1). Have the ball bounce twice on your opponent's end, the second bounce being as close to the end line as possible.

In contrast, long serves should begin about one to two inches from your end line and land deep into the receiver's court, the outermost one-third of the table (zones 1, 2, and 3). No serves should strike the middle one-third of your opponent's table (zones 4, 5, and 6, shaded). (When practicing serves alone, place a towel over this middle one-third so you will easily notice poorly placed balls.)

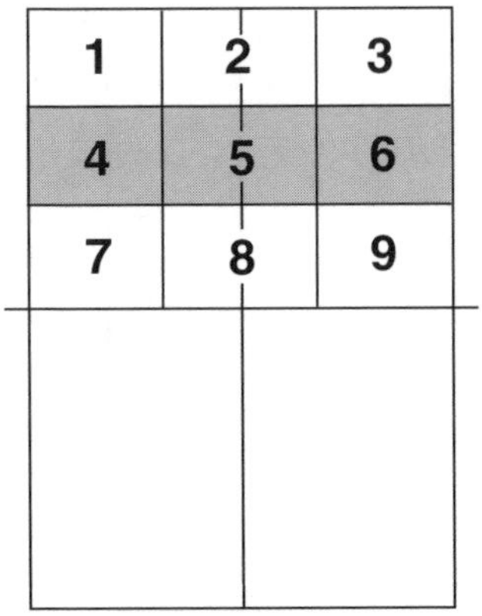

Figure 2.1 Proper zones for service placement. Effective long serves should land in zones 1, 2, and 3; effective short serves, in zones 7, 8, and 9. Never land the ball in the middle three zones.

Vary the amount of wrist you use to change the spin and speed of each serve. For effectiveness and deception, employ many different types of spin from the same look. To maximize the amount of spin, catch and graze the ball at the farthest end of the bat with a mighty snap of your wrist. For less spin, strike the ball nearer to the handle. On some serves, you ought to be able to impart heavy underspin, light underspin, no spin, and even light topspin. No-spin serves, mixed with spin serves, are particularly troublesome for offensive-minded players in today's game.

Of the great number of serves (and limitless variations of them) utilized in play today, space prohibits us from illustrating more than a handful. In what follows, we present some of the most effective and commonly used serves in elite play today.

Forehand Serves From the Backhand Corner

Forehand serves are used almost exclusively by world-class players today. They are very effective because they allow you to initiate the forehand attack easily. First, using more wrist and arm motion, they allow a greater range of motion. Second, after serving forehand, you are better prepared to initiate the attack with your forehand.

Backhand-Corner Forehand-Slice Serve.   The most popular serve used today is the forehand serve from the backhand corner, using right-to-left sidespin. By "right to left," as figure 2.2 illustrates, we mean the

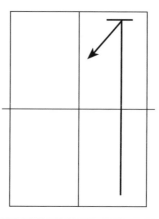

Figure 2.2   Right-to-left sidespin. When you impart right-to-left sidespin on the ball, it will spin off an opponent's neutral paddle and veer toward the left side of your end of the table.

server strikes the ball in a sweeping right-to-left fashion and can expect a return to the left side of the table. The ball itself will spin clockwise. Begin from behind the backhand end and stand with your left shoulder facing your opponent (you will be nearly perpendicular to the table but the left shoulder will be slightly closed). With your left foot at the corner of and perpendicular to the backhand end of the table and the right foot well behind, make a short, eye-level, or high toss. (The higher the toss, the more action on the ball at contact, but the harder it will be to control the serve.)

For the topspin variation, begin with the blade up (at about two o'clock); close your blade somewhat so it is almost perpendicular to the floor. Slide it across the back of the ball and continue up and through the inner side of it. Your playing forearm should contact the ribcage on the right side of your body, stopping abruptly. With the forearm stopped, contact the ball as you begin to draw your elbow back and up, while curling your wrist up and in toward your chin. This imparts top sidespin and slows the forward momentum of the arm as it strikes the ball, allowing maximal spin (see figures 2.3, 2.4, and 2.5).

Figure 2.3 Topspin slice serve, part one.

Figure 2.4   Topspin slice serve, part two.

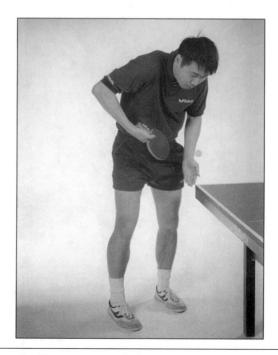

Figure 2.5   Topspin slice serve, part three.

For the underspin variation, begin with the blade up (about two o'clock). Then, keeping it flat, slide it under the ball from right to left. Again, your playing forearm should contact your ribcage. With the forearm stopped, follow through with an upward sweep of the wrist to impart additional underspin (see figures 2.6, 2.7, and 2.8). Throughout, the elbow of your playing arm must stay tight into your body and your bat angle must stay flat—that is, relatively parallel to the floor.

There are two chief benefits of this popular serve. First, by combining sidespin with either topspin or underspin, the receiver has not one, but two reads to make and is more likely to make a mistake on the return. Second, right-to-left sidespin increases the likelihood of a return to the backhand end so you must anticipate which side of the table the ball will strike. As a consequence, this sidespin also makes it hard for the returner to use all parts of the table.

Backhand-Corner Forehand-Hook Serve. A second forehand serve from the backhand end uses left-to-right sidespin—that is, a spin on

Figure 2.6 Underspin slice serve, part one.

Figure 2.7   Underspin slice serve, part two.

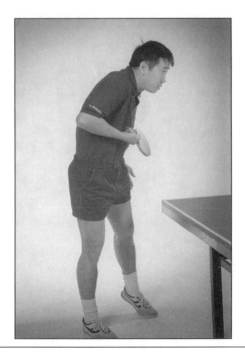

Figure 2.8   Underspin slice serve, part three.

the ball that causes it to veer toward the server's right on the return (see figure 2.9). There are two variations of this difficult serve: one involving topspin, the other using underspin.

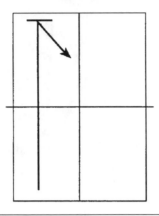

Figure 2.9   Left-to-right sidespin. When you impart left-to-right sidespin on the ball, it will spin off an opponent's neutral paddle and veer toward the right side of your end of the table.

The underspin variation begins deep in the backhand corner with your shoulders perpendicular to the table's end and your feet slightly more than perpendicular (your left foot is turned toward the right end of the table). Make a short, controlled toss—from 6 to 12 inches— with your bat, upper arm lifted and roughly parallel to the floor, concealed behind your back. Keep the blade of your racket opened throughout. At the toss, angle your bat downward and toward your body. Then pull your wrist inward, behind your back, so the palm of your hand curls toward your forearm and your racket blade points to your ribcage. From behind your back, cut under the ball, grazing it with a vigorous left-to-right snap of the wrist. Motion here should be mostly from the elbow down; try to freeze your bat-arm shoulder and pivot at the elbow only. For this variation, it is almost as if you are holding a plate of food on your blade that you wish to set spinning in the air without spilling the food. The path of the paddle with this underspin variation nearly describes the bottom of a semicircle (see figures 2.10 and 2.11).

The topspin variation is easier to perform because the blade of your bat is more closed and your shoulder, in addition to your arm and wrist, is free to move. Begin as with the underspin variation, but keep the blade a bit closed. Run across the back right side of the

Figure 2.10   Underspin hook serve, part one.

Figure 2.11   Underspin hook serve, part two.

ball at contact and follow through with an upward snap of the wrist, pointing your bat upward. By adding shoulder motion here, you impart additional spin or speed on the ball. The path traced by the paddle throughout will almost be side semicircular: from behind your back, around your waist, and to the front of your body (see figures 2.12 and 2.13).

Overall, this serve is more difficult to execute than the first and less effective, because of the limited range of shoulder and wrist motion. However, it can be useful if you use the first serve often simply because, by changing the sidespin, you often catch returners off their guard.

Backhand-Corner Forehand Three-Spin Serve. Another forehand serve from the backhand end that is nearly as popular as the forehand slice, but involves no sidespin, has a hidden contact point and involves varying degrees of spin: heavy underspin, light underspin, and no spin. For this serve, position yourself perpendicular to the table's end, just inside the left end of the table with the front of your left shoulder facing the side of the table. Toss the ball to about eye

Figure 2.12   Topspin hook serve, part one.

Figure 2.13   Topspin hook serve, part two.

level, then turn your left shoulder in toward the center of the table, keeping your left arm up after the toss to better conceal the contact point. Contact the ball from behind the left arm and shoot it from beneath the left arm.

The first variation is heavy underspin. Begin with your blade flat and wrist cocked back, and stroke through the bottom of the ball in a perpendicular fashion, contacting the ball as close to the tip of the bat as possible. At contact, snap your wrist to impart additional underspin and finish the swing with the arm curling slightly upward.

Light underspin is the second option. The blade here is less opened and the wrist is less cocked at the start. Swing through the ball in a slightly downward fashion and contact the ball toward the center of the bat, using less wrist and less of a grazing motion. Finish exactly as you did with the heavy underspin.

No spin is the third option (see figures 2.14, 2.15, and 2.16). Here the blade is roughly perpendicular to the table throughout and you use no wrist. Again, swing through the ball with a small downward motion and contact it near the hand to minimize spin. Obviously, there will be no grazing for this variation; the ball comes off the bat

Figure 2.14   Three-spin serve with no spin, part one.

Figure 2.15   Three-spin serve with no spin, part two.

Figure 2.16   Three-spin serve with no spin, part three.

with a nearly imperceptible bump or thud. Follow through by curl-ing your bat upward. In this option, as with the second one, the follow-through is mostly done to confuse it with the heavy underspin type.

When you properly execute this serve, it is extremely difficult for the receiver to get a clean read on the amount of spin on the ball because the contact point is partially obscured. Consequently, return-ers are often hesitant and less aggressive with their return, and this allows you, as a server, an opportunity to begin the attack on the third ball.

Backhand Serves From the Backhand Corner

Though used less at the world-class level than forehand serves from this corner, these serves allow for great control: They are easy to place and keep low over the net.

Backhand-Corner Backhand-Slice Serve.   The first serve is a short underspin and topspin serve that involves left-to-right sidespin. For underspin, begin square to the table, with your left foot a bit in back of the right and your blade as high as your left shoulder. Cut smoothly but quickly across your body, opening the angle between your upper and lower arm as you finish. Keep your racket face opened and break your wrist at contact, then pull upward with your arm slightly after contact to disguise the spin. By pulling the racket across the right side of your body, you also give left-to-right sidespin (see figures 2.17, 2.18, and 2.19).

The topspin version is similar, but utilizes little wrist and arm motion. With a blade face that is slightly opened and turned into the body, pull across and up on the ball, using movement almost exclusively at the shoulder.

This serve is easily controlled and low risk. It is good if you have a strong forehand or prefer to play the forehand, because the left-to-right sidespin will enable you to play a forehand.

Figure 2.17 Backhand-slice serve with left-to-right sidespin, part one.

Figure 2.18   Backhand-slice serve with left-to-right sidespin, part two.

Figure 2.19   Backhand-slice serve with left-to-right sidespin, part three.

Backhand-Corner Backhand Three-Spin Serve. The fifth serve we illustrate is mechanically similar to the last. However, like the forehand three-spin from the backhand end, it involves no sidespin and has three kinds of spin: heavy underspin, light underspin, and no spin. For heavy underspin, begin with your blade at less than shoulder level and opened, with your wrist cocked. Snap forcibly under the ball at contact, grazing as much as possible, and finish forward. For light underspin, do not graze the ball and snap your wrist so much at contact. The no-spin variety (see figures 2.20, 2.21, and 2.22) has a contact point closer to your hand, with no grazing and no wrist involved.

Use this serve if you like to play your backhand as much as your forehand, because the lack of sidespin allows for an easier backhand opening shot—that is, you do not have to fight your own sidespin preparing for a backhand opening.

Given what we said about ball-placement zones for serving, there are numerous variations of each serve. For instance, the backhand three-spin has eighteen variations: You may serve each of the three spins to the six different placement areas.

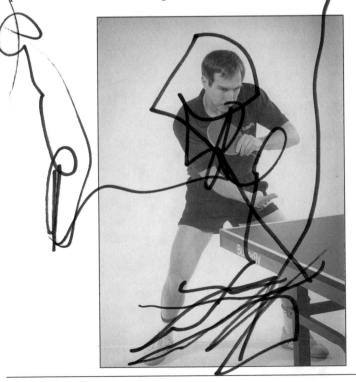

Figure 2.20   Backhand three-spin serve with no spin, part one.

Figure 2.21   Backhand three-spin serve with no spin, part two.

Figure 2.22   Backhand three-spin serve with no spin, part three.

Due to limited space, there are other serves we have not discussed and many service techniques players employ that allow subtle and effective kinds of spin and speed changes. These you may learn simply from observing others or experimenting on your own.

Key Points

1. Vary your service motion and the spin and speed you impart on the ball.
2. For effective deep serves, place the ball in your opponent's last one-third of the table (the deeper, the better).
3. For effective short serves, place the ball in your opponent's first one-third of the table (so if the ball should go unstruck, it would either bounce twice on your opponent's side or barely clear that end of the table.
4. Practice keeping all serves as close to the net as possible.
5. Serve to set up point-winning shots.

SERVICE RETURN

As difficult as it is to practice serves and use them effectively in competitions, service return is the hardest task you face as a table-tennis player. Although the server decides spin, speed, and ball placement, as a returner you must be neutral, trying not to anticipate any serve or placement. You must know your options in advance and be ready for many possibilities, and the best servers disguise their serves well.

To be able to return serves well, in a moment you must read the type and quantity of spin imparted on the ball, the speed at which it travels, its placement, and its depth. Of course, because so many variables are involved in so short a time, this is generally impossible. Misreads at all levels of play are common. This is what gives the server such a huge advantage in playing for the point. Nevertheless, the task is not hopeless; we can give a few guidelines for effective service return that will minimize the serving advantage.

Preparing to Return

When preparing to return, assume the ready position, generally a neutral crouch in your backhand end (see chapter three), and prepare for all reasonable options. The crouch here is especially important because serves have a lower trajectory (they are the only strokes that bounce on *both* sides of the table), and you need to be low to the table to receive them correctly. As your opponents serve, pay attention to their arm motion, especially the wrist, and the sound of the ball at contact. How much arm and wrist motion do they use to generate additional racket speed at contact? Is the direction of motion at contact forward or sideways, under, behind, or on top of the ball? For example, a ball grazed by the tip of the bat with much arm and wrist motion at contact will produce maximal spin on the ball, but not much speed. The same serve, not grazed, will jump off the bat with great speed and little spin. Concerning the sound of the ball at contact, do you hear a loud thud or a quieter, slicing sound? Competitive conditions, because of the noise levels, often make it difficult to discriminate between these two, but it is not impossible. The sound of the ball at contact will be a more reliable indicator of the amount of spin and speed than the visual cues you perceive. As a rule, never commit until you have a good idea of the spin of the serve, and its direction and length.

Rules for All Styles of Returning

The first and most important rule is this: The surest way for you to grasp the intricacies of service return is to learn a full range of serves yourself. By being able to competently perform the different types of serves—with their various spins, speeds, and placements—you gain a practical understanding of them and become a better returner.

Due to the complexity of today's serves, misreads are common and happen even to the best players. Our second rule for improved returning is do not get frustrated when you misread a serve. Instead, gather yourself. Figure out why the mistake occurred and try to adjust.

Third, try to have more than one response to a given serve. This does not mean that you have to use all of these options in a match. If one type of return against a particular serve proves effective in winning or setting up points, there is no need to go away from it. Nevertheless, do not become too predictable. This can be a disadvantage, especially in the late stages of a match. Like new serves, you can think up new returns, or you can learn return options by watching others play who have fluid, creative, and effective returns.

Fourth, do not push too much when returning serves. Today's game is offensive. Pushing, especially when you use it as your only return option, is extremely vulnerable due to its conservativeness. If you are an up-and-coming player, experiment with riskier, aggressive topspin options. If you do not, in the long run your lack of aggressiveness will keep you from becoming a strong returner and a top-level player.

Rules for Aggressive Returning

As the server contacts the ball, you need to make three judgments almost instantaneously. You must determine the type of spin used (side underspin, side topspin, no spin, straight underspin, etc.). You must also judge how much spin is on the serve. To be able to make a return that is low to the net, this read is critical. Last, it is necessary to judge the length of the serve before you choose an appropriate and effective return.

As an offensive player, learn to attack long serves with topspin counters or loops: Counter or lightly loop long topspin serves, loop long underspin or no-spin serves. Servers challenge you with long serves, for the most part, to test your ability to attack them. Being unable to attack long serves enables servers to initiate a strong attack themselves. Long serves, returned nonaggressively, become long returns that are easily attacked on the third ball. Against a long return, servers have additional time to set up for a powerful drive. By establishing a successful attack off these serves, you neutralize their attack, forcing them to serve shorter to begin an attack.

Next, against long serves, do not contact the ball early. Let the ball fall from the top of its bounce and make your return from there. By waiting you have more time to read the ball's speed and spin and you have less speed and spin with which to deal.

For an effective return against short underspin serves, drop the ball short over the net or topspin with a quick flick of the wrist. By dropping the ball close to the net you give servers a dose of their own medicine: They receive a very short underspin ball that is difficult to attack. The quick flick shot is riskier than the drop. Use it against short underspin serves that are high over the net or as an alternative to the drop shot. A mix of these two returns will keep servers off balance.

To return a sidespin serve, contact either the outside or inside of the ball, depending on the spin. The movement of the server's' racket dictates the type of sidespin. As a receiver, movement from right to left means that the ball, when contacting your bat, will spin to your right; movement from left to right will spin the ball to your left.

Last, return short topspin or no-spin serves with long topspin. A push against such a serve often results in a ball that pops up high over the net, one that the receiver can easily smash. In addition, unlike topspin balls, which skip forward after striking the table, underspin balls tend to remain close to the net, sometimes bouncing nearly straight up.

Key Points

1. Assume the ready position and prepare for all reasonable options.
2. Have more than one response to each serve.
3. Learn to return serves aggressively, pushing only for variety.
4. Most importantly, learn to execute the serves that give you trouble.

Chapter 3

Footwork

The 1992 Olympic silver medalist, Jean-Philippe Gatien, shows foot placement and weight shift for the forehand-slice serve from his own backhand end.

*B*ecause table tennis is one of the fastest and most powerful games in the world, it is essential for offensive-minded players to

have exceptional footwork. Stroking techniques will be of little benefit if you are constantly in the wrong position to utilize them. A
strong forehand loop will do you no good when you, anticipating a
deep push to your backhand, are unable to maneuver yourself
quickly to your backhand court for the shot. Consequently, if you
truly wish to be among the game's elite players, you must be capable of quick and efficient movements laterally and toward and
away from the table. If you are incapable of such movements, you
will never be able to play the game as it *should* be played.

THE READY POSITION

Overall, the aim of proper footwork is to enable you to be in the
correct position, the ready position for each shot. By being in position, you give yourself more time to prepare for a shot; you will
make a sounder shot, and you will be better able to use the whole
table. Due to the speed of the game, this is obviously impossible
much of the time. However, by being in the ready position as frequently as possible, you will hit crisper, cleaner shots more often
than your opponents. Moreover, by being set for any one shot, you
are more likely to be in the ready position for the next.

The ready position is not any one place, but the place that puts
you in the best position to cover your opponent's shot, whether you
are positioned for a serve or for a return of one of your serves or
shots. As such, it is determined by the shot or sequence of shots
leading up to it.

Against serves, the ready position is determined by your
opponent's position at the table and, to a lesser extent, both their
and your style of play. Because most offensive players serve primarily from their backhand corner these days, this means that against
serves you will favor your backhand corner most of the time, especially if you are an offensive-minded player.

To illustrate, let us consider two right-handed players, player X
and his opponent, player Y, as shown in figure 3.1. As player Y readies to serve from her backhand court, her position at the table and
the types of serves for which she is noted will determine X's position
for receiving at his end of the table. Assuming Y has a full array of
serves, the angle LCR will roughly describe that part of the table on
which the serve will strike. Therefore, X will position himself some-
where within this angle. This position will always be much toward

his backhand end of the table, toward L, favoring the crosscourt side of the angle. (As a rule of thumb, whenever servers position themselves one foot inside their backhand line, position yourself exactly one foot inside your backhand line. When they position themselves at the middle line, station yourself at the middle line, and so on.)

The situation is the same when readying yourself during a rally. In summary, when preparing to return either a serve or a shot during a rally, your position will be primarily determined by and symmetrical to your opponent's position.

When you find the ready position, stay balanced and poised, just as a hockey goalie in front of a net. Keep your feet slightly farther than shoulder-width apart, with your knees comfortably bent, your head erect, and your weight mostly on the balls of your feet. Point both arms toward your opponent so the angle between your lower and upper arm is approximately 90 degrees (see figure 3.2). Point your bat at your opponent, being wholly indifferent to the expectation of a forehand or backhand shot. In such a manner, you will be prepared for sudden and explosive movements either forward and backward or laterally. Always attempt to ready yourself after each shot, though this is not always possible when you find yourself in awkward positions between shots. If you find yourself in too irregular a position after a shot, do your best to regain lost balance and prepare for a return.

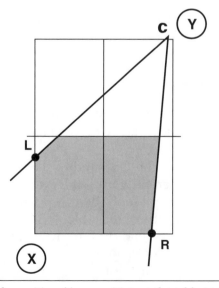

Figure 3.1 The ready position. Your position at the table is determined by your opponent's. Here X readies himself to receive Y's serve.

Figure 3.2   Ready position.

FOOTWORK TECHNIQUES

There are four primary footwork techniques you must learn to have quick and efficient movements at your end of the table.

The Lateral Two-Step

The lateral two-step is a short-distance footwork technique. It enables you to move quickly and with good balance from one side of the table to the other.

To move quickly from the forehand to the backhand side, begin from the forehand corner, lift your left leg so it just clears the floor, then push off with the right foot. (By this push you carry and plant your left foot on the left side of the table.) With the momentum from the initial thrust, bring your right foot over until it nearly hits the heel of the left and set it down. Remember, here the feet do *not* cross over. Last, move the left foot outward so you are in a balanced position. You are now prepared to hit from the backhand corner.

To move back to the forehand side of the table, do exactly the reverse. Push off with the left foot and bring the right foot to the right side. After bringing the left foot to the heel of the right, move the right foot out and ready yourself. You are now prepared to hit from the forehand side of the table (see figure 3.3).

The Up-and-Back Two-Step

The up-and-back two-step allows you to change your depth position as needed. It helps you to move efficiently either away from the table, if you are at the table and being attacked, or toward the table, if you are away from the table and have to move forward. When at the forehand end of the table and preparing to move back to play a forehand, lift your right foot off the floor. With the left foot anchored, move the right back. Then, move your left foot behind the right. Last, move the right foot about a foot behind the left (see figure 3.4). You are now set for a forehand shot. Movement toward the table to play a forehand is merely the reverse of this.

At the backhand side, the movement is similar when moving away from the table, but the right foot is even with or slightly in front of the left at the start. First, lift your left foot off the floor and push off with the right, moving your left leg back. With your left foot planted, move the right foot behind the left. Anchor it, then follow by moving the left behind the right. You are now set for a backhand shot away from the table. The amount of space covered by each step will be determined by the total space you need to cover.

Movement toward the table will be exactly the reverse of this.

The Backhand-Corner Two-Step

This movement is almost the same as the lateral two-step. Here, however, the object is to enable you to play your forehand from your backhand side. Forehand attack shots from the backhand corner are the most effective attack shots in the game. To play a forehand when standing deep within the backhand corner, two-step past the left end of the table so the front of your body is nearly parallel to the table's side and perpendicular to its end (see figure 3.5). The footwork here is the same as in the lateral two-step. The only difference is that you are not moving laterally, but curling around the end of the table, moving both sideways and up. You are now in position for a forehand attack from deep within the backhand corner.

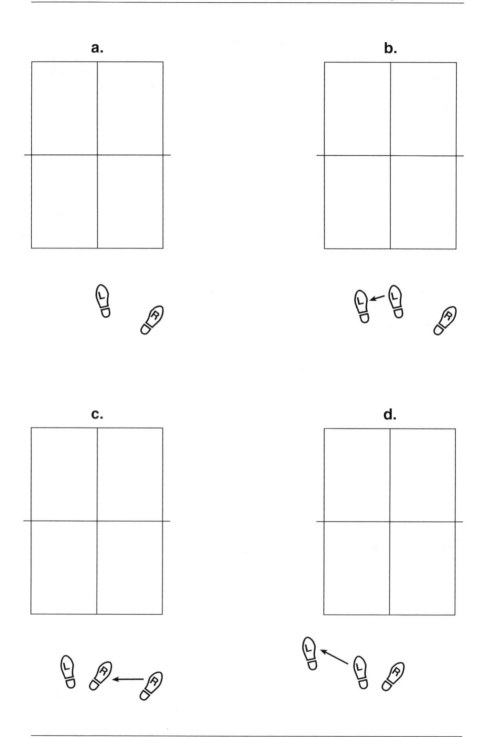

Figure 3.3   Lateral two-step.

a.

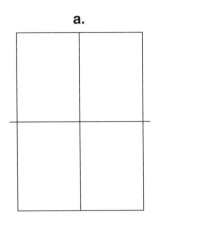

b.

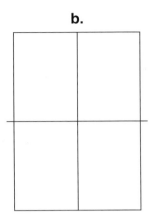

c.

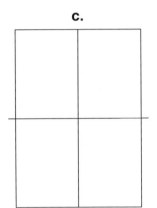

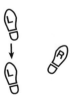

d.

Figure 3.4 Up-and-back two-step.

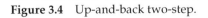

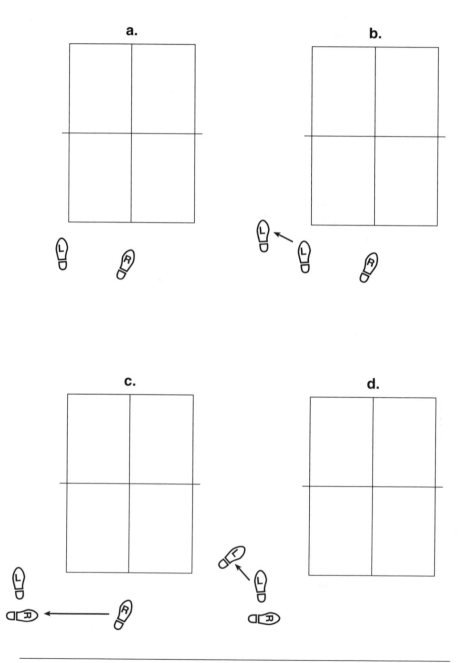

Figure 3.5   Backhand-corner two-step.

To return to a set position in the backhand corner, simply two-step back. Because this footwork takes you around the backhand end of the table (both back and to the right), the footwork combines elements of the lateral two-step and the front-and-back two-step.

Overall, learning to play a forehand from the backhand corner is important because the table is not in the way (you may move up past the end of the table) and, therefore, you have a fuller and surer hit from this spot. In addition to this, playing one forehand attack shot from the backhand zone makes it easier to maintain a powerful forehand attack.

The Lateral Crossover

The lateral crossover is the most difficult footwork technique to practice and incorporate into a game. Use it only when you need to cover lateral distances over four or five feet quickly.

When moving from deep in the backhand corner to the forehand corner, first step outward as far as comfortably possible to the right with the right leg. Then, after bringing the left leg over and across the front of the right, swing the right leg out from behind the left foot and over as far as comfortably possible to the right. You are now in a position to hit (see figure 3.6).

When moving from the forehand to the backhand side, step outward with the left foot, cross the right behind the left, then throw the left out again to your backhand end so you are in a set position in the backhand corner.

By learning the four types of footwork illustrated, you will be capable of fast and efficient movements toward, away from, and to both sides of the table. Practice these first by yourself. Try footwork drills with a practice partner only when you are comfortable with the movements. Footwork drills, which we illustrate in chapter six, are indispensable for elite play because they teach you what stroking drills (again in chapter six) and footwork alone cannot: how to incorporate movement with sound mechanical stroking. This is the essence of match play and the reason so many players with exceptional strokes never make it to the elite level.

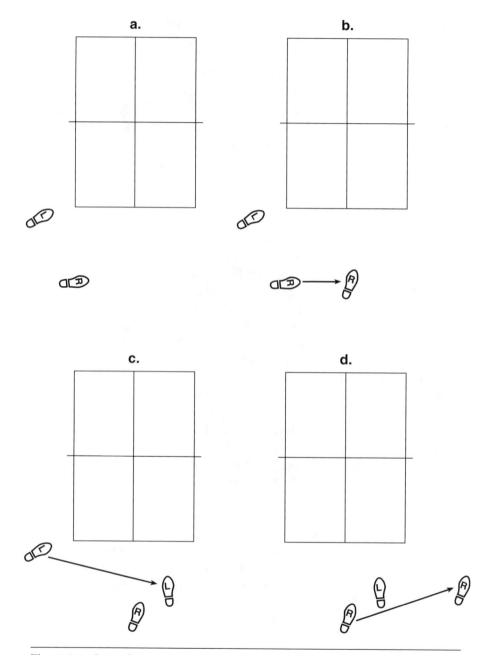

Figure 3.6 Lateral crossover.

Part II

PREPARING TO PLAY

Csilla Batorfi draws up a serve at the 1995 World Team Cup.

Chapter 4

Choosing the Right Equipment

China's Deng Yaping, 1992 Olympic gold medalist, with impeccable execution of a forehand smash.

There are a few questions you should ask yourself before selecting table-tennis equipment. What is my level of play? What is my style of play? Are there any physical reasons why some equipment suits me better than other equipment? In this chapter, we look at the most basic equipment of the game—the blade, the rubber, and table-tennis dress—and offer some guidelines for selecting wisely.

THE BLADE

In choosing a blade, there are many factors that come into play: weight, size, shape, material, feel, handle. (We treat rubber in the following section.)

Blade Weight

Bat weight is a combination of the size of the blade, its thickness, its material, and the density of the material. In general, the lighter the blade, the easier its mobility and the greater the velocity of the paddle on impact. Such blades are ideal for hitters who play up at the table and need to move quickly and decisively. In contrast, a heavier paddle allows more dynamic topspin on loops, more stability on blocks, and usually greater speed on the ball. (A heavier blade swung at the same velocity as a lighter one transfers more energy at contact.) We recommend that you use as heavy a blade as is comfortable. Remember however, that the type and thickness of the rubber you choose along with a blade will dramatically affect the overall weight of the paddle. Take a few swings with paddles used by members at your local club before purchasing a blade, or get advice from a local distributor.

Blade Size and Shape

The size and shape of the paddle are a matter of your style of play. Defensive players, who win by frustrating you and forcing you into errors, mostly prefer a larger blade so there is little chance of misconnecting with a shot. Aggressive players prefer smaller blades because, having less air resistance, they can swing them faster. Concerning shape, a rounded blade is good for overall control and almost any style of play. A thin and elongated blade allows maximal spin on both serves and loops when you contact the ball near the head and use plenty of wrist.

Blade Material

There are only two choices of material for today's blades: all wood or an admixture of wood and carbon. The wooden blades range from one to nine plies and offer a variety of speed and control combinations. The number, thickness, and distribution of plies affect the speed and control of the ball. The carbon blades tend to be faster and less spinny with larger sweet spots, but are two to two and one-half times the price of the wooden ones.

Blade Feel

Another important factor in choosing a blade is its feel. The feel of a blade is more than how it sits in your playing hand; it has to do as well with how solidly the ball leaves your racket blade at contact and how far this solid feeling extends throughout the blade. Consequently, the feel of a blade involves both its weight distribution and its sweet spot. Regarding the former, loopers may want a top-heavy feel to their paddles. Defensive players, desiring more control, may opt for more weight in the handle. Concerning the sweet spot, before buying a blade, drop a ball from a given height on several parts of the blade while holding it firmly in your playing hand. If you notice the solid feeling only around the center of the blade, it has a small sweet spot. If this feeling extends almost to all ends of the blade, it has a large sweet spot. A large sweet spot is always preferable to a small one regardless of your style of play.

Blade Handle

There are four standard handle types for the shakehands style of play: straight, flared, conic, and anatomic (see figures 4.1, 4.2, 4.3, and 4.4). There are arguments put forth by those who prefer one over the others, but none of these seem convincing to us. We suggest that you decide for yourself by getting a feel for each.

THE RUBBER

Tailor the type and thickness of the rubber you choose to the type of game you play.

Rubber Types

Inverted, antispin, pips-out, and long-pips rubbers are the most common types. Inverted rubbers are smooth faced and grippy,

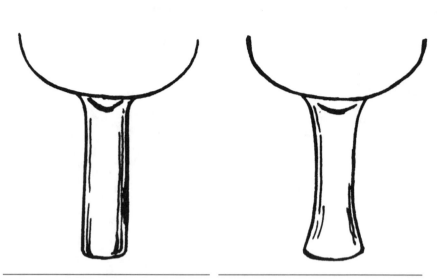

Figure 4.1   Straight handle.

Figure 4.2   Conic handle.

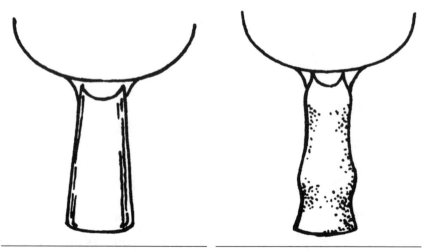

Figure 4.3   Flared handle.

Figure 4.4   Anatomic handle.

generally good attack rubbers that allow for maximal speed and spin. If your game is hitting, the one and one-half or two millimeter thickness is best. As a looper, you may prefer to cover both sides with a two millimeter rubber or, if you are a predominantly forehand looper, you may wish to cover your forehand with two and one-half millimeter rubber, the maximum thickness allowed, and your backhand with two.

Antispin rubbers are inverted but not grippy. They impart very little spin and speed and are generally used if you have a defensive posture. Because they generate little spin and speed, antispin rubbers are most effective when playing against those who use heavy spin or hit fast. Against heavy spin, the ball does not grip but slips off and returns the opposite spin to the spinner. Defensive players with this rubber usually try to wear their opponents down with the opponent's own spin.

If your rubber type is inverted, before and after play clean the rubber surface of your bat regularly with water. Occasionally use a bit of soap to break down any skin oils that may have accumulated from prolonged play.

Pips-out rubbers or "short pips" are mostly controlled attack rubbers. With the pips out, the speed of the ball is slightly faster and the amount of spin on the ball is much less than inverted rubbers. Therefore, heavily spun shots are less effective against short pips. This is an ideal rubber for quick attackers who play close to the table.

Long pips, like antispin rubber, is a defensive rubber that creates little speed and spin of its own, though more than the antispin. It differs from antispin in that it is *really* troublesome against heavy topspinners. The bending of the pips allows for a truer return of spin so a heavily topspun ball can come back with severe underspin. Impatient attackers will be overpowered by their own spin.

Rubber Thickness

Rubbers come in four standard thicknesses. The thicker the rubber, the faster it is and the more difficult it is to control. One millimeter thickness is the thinnest and slowest, best for control. One and one-half millimeter thickness allows more speed with a slight loss of control. Two millimeter thickness, the most popular, is even faster and is a sound choice for an aggressive style of play. Two and one-half millimeter rubber is the fastest available, but is more difficult to control.

DRESSING FOR PLAY

Of what you wear, your shoes are the most important item. Worn-out shoes or those with poor cushion greatly stress your hips, knees, ankles, and feet, and 90 percent of all sports injuries occur in these areas. Replace your shoes often; in just a few months, they can lose one-third of their shock-absorbing capacity. Running shoes offer no lateral support, so are inadequate for table tennis. Volleyball and racketball shoes, because they allow better support, are best for cushioning your feet on hard surfaces like cement; for wooden or rubbered floors, the thinner-soled table-tennis shoes of most manufacturers may be adequate.

Regarding other sportswear, wear shorts and a shirt that allow comfortable movement. Otherwise, dress according to the environment. In a hot environment, dress coolly so your perspiration may evaporate easily. Change sweaty clothes as frequently as possible. For competitions, use two towels at a table: one for your playing hand, the other for your body. In a cool environment, change sweaty clothes and wear a warm-up suit when you are not playing.

Chapter 5

Training Preparation and Care

Alan Cooke of England with a forehand loop drive at the 1995 Sears International Tournament in Palatine, Illinois.

*I*ntense daily training puts a great strain on your body. Continued strain leads inevitably to overtraining, fatigue, and sometimes burnout. As a serious player you must do everything you can to get (and keep) your body in peak shape and to recuperate from session to session. You must get adequate rest between workouts, replace the nutrients lost in them, use methods that help your muscles recover faster, and do whatever is in your power to avoid injury. These components of training are every bit as important as the daily practice sessions and mental preparation strategies you go through to get the most of your table-tennis talent.

In what follows we discuss various pre- and postexercise ways of getting the most out of your training. These include specific suggestions on proper warm-up, means of facilitating quicker recovery from workout to workout, finding your correct playing weight, nutritional intake and improved performance, and sleep needs.

WARMING UP

The first thing you should do to prepare yourself for a training session or tournament is warm up. A good warm-up elevates your heart rate and increases blood flow and respiration. This, in turn, increases the temperature of your muscles, tendons, and ligaments and reduces the likelihood of a sprain or tear when playing. Warming up makes oxygen more accessible to your muscle cells, which is beneficial just before play. It may also prevent injury and lessen muscle soreness. Stretching after exercise is a way for you to cool down, increase flexibility, and prevent injury and muscle soreness.

In what follows, we break warming up into three parts: prestretch warm-up, stretching, and sport-specific warm-up. Before any serious workout or tournament, follow a strict warm-up procedure in just this manner.

Prestretch Warm-Up

The prestretch warm-up should consist exclusively of some light cardiovascular work designed to elevate your heart rate and increase respiration slightly. Jogging in place, a light run, or some nonrigorous calisthenics are sufficient. A light sweat is a suitable indicator that you have completed this phase of your warm-up. Prestretch warm-up should take no longer than five minutes.

Stretching

After the prestretch warm-up, allow yourself 15 to 20 minutes for stretching. Table tennis utilizes all the major muscle groups. Therefore, you should stretch each of these muscles thoroughly before you begin play. If you spend less time, then you are likely neglecting certain key muscle groups.

Follow two specific rules for maximum benefits of each stretch. First, perform each stretch slowly, so the stretching feels relaxed and not strained. Second, as you stretch a muscle to its fullest, hold this position for a count of 20, slightly relax the stretch without getting out of the stretch position, then try to stretch the muscle even more for another count of 20. Repeat this for a total of three times, while concentrating on improving the amount of stretch each time.

In what follows, we illustrate 14 stretches, all of which you should perform before each training session or tournament and, whenever possible, afterward. We start with large or significant muscle groups, then work our way to the remaining relevant muscles.

Groin Stretch. In a sitting position on the floor, bring the feet together into the groin so the bottoms of the feet touch each other. With the knees flared outward, slowly press down on the inner part of each knee with your elbows while holding the feet together with your hands (see figure 5.1). Hold this position for a count of 20 when fully stretched, relax the stretch for a few seconds, then repeat for a total of three stretches.

Figure 5.1 Groin stretch.

Hamstring Stretch. Place the leg you are stretching on an elevated surface such as the table. Keeping that leg straight (there should be no bending at the knee), bring the head slowly toward the knee while breathing out and hold for a count of 20 after no further stretch is possible. Relax the stretch while maintaining the stretch position and breath normally for a few seconds, then repeat this stretch two more times, each time trying to stretch farther without sacrificing good form. Work the unstretched leg next.

Quadriceps Stretch. In a standing position, with the right hand, grab the front of the ankle from behind and slowly pull upward as far as possible so the heel of the foot touches the right buttock. Hold this position, then work the left leg. Repeat for three stretches.

Obliques Stretch. Place the right hand on the right side of the neck and the left hand on the left side of the waist. Standing perfectly erect, move the upper body as far to the left as possible while keeping the lower body still. The right side of the waist should feel fully stretched. Alternate for the left side. Hold and repeat for each side.

Abdominal Stretch. Standing erect with your hands behind your head, move the upper body as far backward as possible while trying to keep the lower body motionless. The abdominals should be bowed forward and fully stretched. Hold and repeat.

Lower-Back Stretch. Sit on the floor with legs slightly spread and extended in front of the body, hands around your ankles, and bring the head as close to the floor as possible. Keep your knees slightly bent throughout this stretch (for this is not a hamstring stretch), and maintain this bend to keep the hamstrings out of play. Hold and repeat.

Upper-Back Stretch. Take hold of a pole or any other fixed vertical object with the right hand. Cross the left arm over the right and pull as far as possible, until the right upper latt feels fully stretched (see figure 5.2). Stretch for a count of 20. Alternate arms, hold, and repeat.

Chest Stretch. Lean the right forearm along some fixed object like a wall or pole. Lean forward slowly and stretch the arm back until the right pectoral is fully stretched. Stretch the left pectoral next, then repeat.

Figure 5.2   Upper-back stretch.

Shoulder Stretches.   Stretch one. Standing erect under a doorway, lean both forearms across the top of the doorway, then lean forward, trying not to bend the arms. Hold, then repeat two more times.

Stretch two (see figure 5.3). Hold both arms straight out from the back of the body, resting them against some stationary object so the arm to lower-body angle is roughly 90 degrees. Stretch the shoulders by either moving the body forward or squatting downward so the angle from the lower body to the arms increases. (If no appropriate object is available, a friend may oblige by offering resistance.) Hold and repeat.

Calf and Ankle Stretches.   There are four stretches in all. Cross the right leg over the left. Holding the foot with both hands, stretch the top of the foot toward the front of the leg (stretch one), the bottom of the foot toward the back of the leg (stretch two), the left side of the foot toward the left side of the right leg (stretch three), then the right side of the foot toward the right side of the right leg (stretch four). Alternate legs and repeat.

Figure 5.3   Shoulder stretch, stretch two.

Neck Stretches.   There are four separate, easy neck stretches. First, with both hands behind the neck, slowly press the front of the head downward toward the chest. Next, press the back of the head toward the back. Third, press the left side of the head down to the left shoulder. Do the same for the right side of the head. Hold, then repeat two times.

Wrist and Forearm Stretches.   There are four more stretches here. Holding the right hand in the left, push the top of the right hand back toward the top of the right forearm. Next, push the palm of the hand toward the bottom of the forearm. Last, stretch each side of the forearm.

Spinal Stretch.   Merely hang by your hands from a pole or door for a count of at least 30. This allows the spine to fully stretch and relaxes the pressure on the spinal disks, which take a beating in daily training. Do only one set here, both before and after training.

Sport-Specific Warm-Up

After stretching, begin your sport-specific warm-up to prepare you for practice or actual play. This type of warm-up gives you all the benefits of the prestretch warm-up, plus it allows you to prepare effectively for actual play by utilizing the muscles in a way that mimics actual play. (Notice that professionals of all sports warm up in this way.) Here, do a few minutes of shadow stroking (practice stroking without a ball), some shadow footwork drills by the end of a table, then mimic a few game-situation volleys in a similar way. Perform these movements unhurriedly at first, but gradually approach the intensity and speed of actual match play by the end of this warm-up. Much more than with the prestretch phase, perform the sport-specific warm-up with great focus on detail and energy. After a few minutes of this, begin practice.

EXERCISE RECOVERY

Athletic conditioning is a continual process of muscular breaking down and building up. To maintain or improve conditioning, the amount of rebuilding you do must *at least* equal the amount of breaking down that your daily workouts do. If the breakdown you do to your muscle tissue constantly exceeds your body's capacity to build back up, your conditioning slows and eventually deteriorates. In this section we concentrate on the regenerative phase of conditioning and suggest ways of improving workout recovery.

Passive and Active Recovery

We can break down workout recovery into two forms: passive and active recovery. Passive recovery is merely inactivity. To recover passively, simply do nothing after a training session, let the body heal itself by its own capacities, and return to training when you are fully recovered. This is the traditional method of recovery preferred by most athletes of all sports and certainly an important aspect of the recuperative phase.

However, at the elite level of athletic competition, passive recovery is inadequate. After a table-tennis tournament or an intense practice session, not only does muscle tissue break down, glycogen (your body's most accessible fuel source) is also depleted. In all, full recovery may take up to 48 hours. By continually working intensely on a daily basis, your body, through passive recovery, is not able to repair all the damage you do to it. As an elite or aspiring table-tennis player, you need to practice active recovery.

Active recovery is what you can do to promote and advance healing beyond your body's capacity to heal itself. Active recovery promotes quicker healing by exceeding the recuperative effects of passive recovery. There are many standard methods of promoting active recovery. Stretching immediately after exercise improves circulation. In this manner, oxygen and glycogen are more freely carried to muscle tissue and lactic acid (a metabolic by-product of exercise that causes soreness) is better carried away from it. Saunas and steam baths loosen the muscles and bring relief from tension. Deep massage relaxes the body and, like stretching, promotes circulation in the muscle tissue. Replacing fluids and carbohydrates also speeds recovery. (We give a detailed account of fluid and carbohydrate replacement in chapter eight.) If you wish to have the most efficient and intense workouts for which you are capable, practice active recovery methods.

Supplementing Recovery Methods

In spite of active methods of recovery, you may still experience muscle soreness regularly. Constantly working out with sore muscles is harmful and a sure sign of overtraining—that is, training with muscles that have not fully recovered from prior workouts. One way around this is to train only when your muscles are not sore. Yet, this is a strategy that will leave you, as a table-tennis player, training no more than every other day—a strategy certain to keep you from your best. If you train daily, you need to diversify your sessions.

Through diversified training, you vary the intensity and duration of your workout sessions. When your playing shoulder and legs are overly sore from excessive looping or smashing drills done on Monday, spend Tuesday focusing on serves or simpler, less-exertive drills. By Wednesday (or Thursday at the latest), the soreness will be gone. Through getting to know your body, you will be able to plan the length and intensity of your training sessions. We have more to say on diversified training in our section on cycle training in chapter eight.

In addition, vigorous exercise produces greater and lengthier muscle soreness in unconditioned athletes. If you are just beginning to earnestly train for table tennis or if you are resuming a training regimen after having been away from the game for some time, you can minimize muscle soreness by easing into your training sessions. However, even if you choose not to ease into your training, the soreness will gradually disappear with continued training.

Also, because the mental aspects of intense training are significant, for overall physical recovery, practice mental relaxation. Mental relaxation brings about reduced psychological stress. Without it, the intense mental preparation and tension of serious training and competing will take its toll and eventually you will burn out. Periodically do things to take your mind off the game. Read a classic by Dickens or a poem by Li Po. Take a long walk or rent a video. In short, do whatever it is that relaxes you and regenerates interest in table tennis. At times, if your desire for the game seems spent, take a break from it, anywhere from a few days to a week or two, and do absolutely nothing directly related to the sport. Concentrate on running or lifting weights, or just do nothing at all. Periodic breaks are essential for keeping up interest in table tennis and maintaining peak training intensity.

OPTIMAL BODY COMPOSITION

Peak athletic performance in all sports, and table tennis is no exception, is greatly improved by optimal body composition. As a table-tennis player, you may bring about significant improvement in your table-tennis game by improving your conditioning through diet and exercise.

Keep your body fat at a low but healthy percentage. The reason is simple. Percentage of body fat is a reliable barometer of athletic success in any sport. If you carry more fat around than you need, your performance will fall off. You become a slower and less efficient athlete. Imagine trying to play your normal game of table tennis with a 20-pound weight strapped to your body. The results would assuredly be catastrophic. This is roughly what happens when you carry 20 more pounds of fat than you need.

Moreover, body fat increases body temperature while exercising. First, fat insulates and keeps body heat inside. Second, with fat being approximately 50 percent water and muscle being around 75 percent water, a body with less muscle and more fat has less water for cooling purposes. The moral is simply this: To play the best game of table tennis you can possibly play, you must lose the excess fat.

The average male has from 13 to 17 percent body fat, and the average female has 20 to 27 percent. Because table tennis combines elements of both aerobic and anaerobic conditioning, we recommend that males strive to have from 8 to 12 percent body fat; females, from 14 to 23 percent. Never strive for near-zero body fat. Remember, fat is a source of energy too, though a secondary one. Too little body fat will leave you with low energy reserves for proper performance.

Although it is critical to have a low percentage of body fat, it is also important to develop the right amount of muscle for table-tennis play. (We talk about ways to improve muscle and strength in chapters seven and eight.) How should you strive to build and distribute your muscle mass for this end? The answer is simple. Look at the better professional players in table tennis and see how they are proportioned. For example, loopers are thicker in the buttocks and thighs than pure hitters, because looping strains the lower-body muscles more than hitting. Choppers are thinner and less powerfully built than other players because their style of play requires more flexibility and endurance, but less power. Once you decide how you should proportion yourself, begin a conditioning program designed to lose the excess fat and build your muscles up to suit your game.

Key Points

1. Strive to keep body fat low: 8 to 12 percent for males, 14 to 23 percent for females.
2. Develop muscle where you need it for your style of play.

THE RIGHT WAY TO LOSE WEIGHT

As we established previously, athletes carrying around more fat than they need are much less efficient than those at optimal playing weight. As a table-tennis player, you should be lean and muscular, with the bulk of your muscle being carried in your legs, hips, and waist. Drop any unneeded body fat. There is a right way and a wrong way to do this.

The first rule is this: There is no easy way to lose unwanted pounds. Crash diets, promising extraordinary weight loss, work by reducing your caloric intake to dangerously low levels. Dieters lose weight quickly, and this seems a happy end. However, what usually happens is that they lose muscle mass while retaining considerable body fat. This is precisely what you as an athlete do not want to do, because it is a course designed to lose a greater proportion of muscle than fat.

The problem is that crash diets are directed toward losing weight, not body fat. If you go about losing weight in the wrong manner, you may actually be a less efficient player *after* the weight loss. Concern yourself, instead, with reducing body fat and keeping as much muscle mass as possible, not merely losing weight. If you are overweight, a sensible goal is to reduce body weight by no more than one-half pound per week. This means that, from a diet designed to maintain your body weight each week, to lose one-half pound you will have to cut out nearly 1,750 calories each week. You can do this by carefully monitoring the calories you eat daily—cutting back or leaving out the least nutritious foodstuffs. For instance, if you like to drink a couple colas every day, you can easily lose one-half pound a week by cutting these out or switching either to diet colas or, better yet, water.

When losing weight, eat mainly complex carbohydrates. These are usually high in fiber and loaded with nutrients. Try as well to maintain protein intake. This means that your weight loss will come primarily at the expense of fat calories (or any alcohol calories you may consume). By such a diet, your energy level will not drop off too much and you will retain almost all of your muscle mass.

Resistance training (for instance, weight lifting) is perhaps the best way to maintain muscle mass while losing weight. If possible, train in the morning. This raises your resting metabolic rate throughout the day so you burn more calories and, in general, function more efficiently. In chapter seven we suggest a weight lifting program for improving overall conditioning. You may use this program when dieting.

Key Points

1. Stay away from crash diets.
2. Lose weight slowly and methodically, ideally at a rate of one pound every two weeks.

NUTRITION

As a serious table-tennis player, you have a high-energy expenditure that requires a high-energy diet. Of the nutrients you consume, only calories give you energy. Proteins, carbohydrates, and fats provide you with nearly all the caloric content in the foods you consume. Consequently, calories fulfill your energy needs. Other nutrients, like vitamins and minerals, though essential for proper bodily functioning, do not give you energy.

Carbohydrates

The most efficient calories are in carbohydrates. Carbohydrates function mostly as short-term fuel for the muscles and the brain. You use them at twice the rate of fats when you exercise intensely, and the quick availability of a fuel source is the most important factor in rating its work-producing efficiency.

Carbohydrates are the primary fuel for glycogen storage. Blood and muscle glycogen serve as the main fuel for muscular performance, especially during intense exercise. Further glycogen is stored in the liver and is used when blood and muscle glycogen stores are depleted.

Because carbohydrates are easily converted to glycogen, as a table-tennis player, roughly 60 percent of your calories should be in carbohydrate form. When in intense training, increase carbohydrate intake to 70 percent of your overall diet, because of the greater need for readily available glycogen. The extra 10 percent should come at the expense of fats. If, for example, you are a 75-kilogram (165-pound) table-tennis player, who trains hard every day, take in anywhere from 370 to 525 grams of carbohydrate per day—that is, 1,480 to 2,100 calories. (Carbohydrates and proteins have four calories per gram; fats have around nine.) The lower end of this scale is preferable, except for days of heavy training or tournaments. Three days before a tournament, load up on carbohydrates, taking up to 80 percent of your total calories in carbohydrates. In this manner, your body will have a superabundance of ready-to-use fuel.

Of the carbohydrates you ingest, eat mostly the complex ones (pastas, breads, cereals, vegetables, certain fruits, and beans) and the rest simple ones (most fruits, certain vegetables, and fruit juices). Why? First, complex carbohydrates quickly pass through the stomach and are unlikely to produce gastrointestinal discomfort. Second, they elevate blood-glycogen levels, but not harmfully like most simple sugars do. By increasing your blood-glycogen levels too rapidly, which the ingestion of simple sugars often does, your pancreas produces insulin to neutralize the excess fuel. This, in turn, prevents the use of fats for energy. In short, complex carbohydrates keep the blood-glycogen levels high enough to give you more fuel, but not so high as to trigger an insulin response. Third, complex carbohydrates are often high in fiber. A high-fiber diet helps to stabilize blood glycogen, keeping blood glycogen from getting too high. Last, complex carbohydrates generally have more vitamins and minerals than simple ones.

Choose carbohydrates mostly from legumes and whole grains. Soybeans, kidney beans, lentils, sweet potatoes, whole grain pastas, brown rice, apples, and whole grain breads are some of the carbohydrate-laden foods you should regularly consume. For fiber, eat foods such as beans, peas, lentils, peanuts, pumpkin seeds, carrots, broccoli, bananas, raisins, raspberries, apples, figs, pears, oats, sweet corn, rye bread, wheat bread, and unbuttered popcorn. Avoid white-floured breads and pastas, and white rice. These foods may initiate an insulin response from the pancreas, causing a reduction of blood glucose.

When taking in carbohydrates in liquid form, choose a fructose-based drink in preference to a glucose-based one. The latter may trigger an insulin response, whereas the former is a safer alternative. Fructose may also function to convert fats to readily available fuel and preserve glycogen.

Proteins

Proteins are the second form of work-producing nutrients. They control all your bodily functions through the activity of enzymes (substances that help to bring about the chemical changes in your body) and comprise over 50 percent of the dry weight in your body. Proteins also build and repair muscle tissue, red blood cells, and other tissues, and synthesize hormones. Therefore, you must consume quality proteins every day, and take them wisely, if you want to play your best table tennis.

The Recommended Dietary Allowance (RDA) for protein intake is .8 grams per kilogram of body weight per day (.8g/kg/day). For example, according to the RDA, our 75-kilogram (165-pound) table-tennis player would need 60 grams of protein daily. The conventional wisdom of recent years has been that serious athletes should ingest "a bit more" than the RDA for restoration and muscle-building purposes, but not much more.

The latest research shows this "wisdom" is anything but wise. Intense exercise causes a significant increase in the rate your body uses protein. Regular moderate exercise for men doubles their protein needs, and the protein needs for intense exercise may be even greater. Our recommendation is that you take in from 1.2 to 1.6 grams per kilogram per day, depending on the amount and intensity of daily practice. However, be careful not to ingest too much protein. Taking in too much protein may saddle you with unneeded calories.

Lean meats—like chicken and venison—and most fishes are quality sources of protein. If possible, buy only fresh meats and fish. Canned tuna, of which albacore or white tuna is best, is a preferred choice of protein among athletes. If you eat meat, avoid red meats altogether because of their high saturated fat content.

An inexpensive alternative to fish and meat is beans and whole grains. Though less-concentrated sources of protein than meat and fish, legumes are high in protein and an excellent source of energy-efficient complex carbohydrates. For example, three and one-half ounces of ground round contain 209 calories, 27.4 grams of protein, zero carbohydrates, and 11.3 grams of artery-clogging fat. In contrast, one-half cup of pinto beans contains 349 calories, 22.9 grams of protein, 63.7 grams of carbohydrate, and only 1.2 grams of fat. The pinto beans are by far the better fuel source because they have more calories, less fat, and an astonishing level of high-quality carbohydrates.

Overall, consume protein in small amounts during the day, no more than 30 grams per sitting.

Fats

Fats are the third work-producing nutrient. Like carbohydrates, fats are an important source of energy during exercise. Light and low-intensity practice sessions of long duration use both fats and carbohydrates as fuel sources. As you practice longer in such sessions, you use fats more and more, as long as the oxygen supply is adequate (and this should be no problem if you are at least moderately fit). When exercise intensity increases, you use less fat. Obviously, table tennis, because it requires both aerobic and anaerobic fitness, is a sport in which you draw from both fat reserves and glycogen stores plentifully.

Fats burn very slowly for energy because your body cannot break fats down as quickly as carbohydrates. Therefore, though denser sources of potential energy, fats are much less efficient fuel sources than carbohydrates. They are utilized primarily when muscle and blood-glycogen levels are in low reserve. Consequently, fats are a last-resort energy source. Limit your fat intake to be a more efficient athlete. Optimally, fat intake should *never* comprise more than 25 to 30 percent of your total calories.

There are other nutrients, which we must neglect here, that may improve your work efficiency: caffeine, creatin, sodium bicarbonate, chromium picolinate, and antioxidants, to name a few. Read the recent literature on such nutrients before spending loads of money on them. Some may prove effective dietary supplements if you learn to take them in the right manner. (For those interested in seeing how protein and carbohydrate intake may be planned for daily professional play, see table 5.1.)

Before we end this section, remember this: Improved nutrition has a critical role in serious athletic performance. When beginning a program to better your diet, be patient! Just as you do not expect to markedly improve your table-tennis game in two or three training sessions, do not expect health and performance benefits in a few days. It may take months to notice the difference, but what a difference it will make! Be persistent, and the payoff will be remarkable.

Table 5.1 Sample Diet for Professional Player

7:15 a.m.:	Wake and eat meal one—25 grams protein, 100 grams carbohydrate.
8:45 a.m.:	Light carbohydrate preworkout meal (meal two)—50 grams.
9:30 a.m.-12:00 p.m.:	Early morning practice session.
12:15 p.m.:	Meal three—25 grams protein, 100 grams carbohydrate.
12:30-2:00 p.m.:	Afternoon nap or rest.
2:15 p.m.:	Light carbohydrate preworkout meal (meal four)—50 grams.
3:00-5:00 p.m.:	Afternoon practice session.
5:15 p.m.:	Meal five—25 grams protein, 100 grams carbohydrate.
7:30-8:30 p.m.:	Evening practice session.
8:45 p.m.:	Meal six—25 grams protein, 100 grams carbohydrate.
2:00 a.m.:	Meal seven—25 grams protein, 100 grams carbohydrate. (If you are very serious about the game, learn to wake yourself for this important meal. Without it, your body goes too long without food, and it takes longer to restore the glycogen levels in the blood and liver to normal upon waking. Taken regularly, this meal will have a noticeable effect on the quality of your early morning workouts.)

Key Points

1. Make sure you take in 60 to 70 percent of your calories in carbohydrate form, mostly complex carbohydrates, depending on the intensity of training.
2. Take in from 1.2 to 1.6 grams of protein per kilogram (2.2 pounds) of body weight each day, no more than 30 grams in one sitting.
3. Keep fat intake low, especially saturated fat.
4. Be persistent with a healthy diet because results will not come overnight.

SLEEP NEEDS

Adequate sleep is essential for good table-tennis play. The harder and more frequently you train, the more sleep you need.

Lack of sleep by itself is often the cause of overtraining and lethargy. At other times it is one of many causes. Furthermore, intense exercise increases the need for the deeper and most vital stages of sleep. One way of getting around these problems is to get enough sleep each day when training.

Length of sleep is correlated with health. To optimize health, the average person needs between seven and eight hours of sleep each night. But, because of the unusual demands placed upon your body as a table-tennis player, your sleep needs are greater than the average person's. When practicing table tennis every day, try to get between eight and nine hours of sleep per night, on average. If you train more than once a day or for more than four hours, incorporate a midday nap into your schedule, if possible. (Keep in mind that these numbers apply to the average person. Sleep needs vary considerably from individual to individual. If you function best with six hours of sleep per day when you are not training intensely, you may need seven or eight hours of sleep when you are in training.)

Key Point

1. Expect your sleep needs to increase during intense training and try to meet these needs with a midday nap, if possible.

Chapter 6

Conditioning Drills

Superbly conditioned Khoa Nguyen of the United States with a strong forehand loop against topspin.

There are numerous components to table-tennis success. On the physical side, they include motor skills, physical conditioning, injury-prevention techniques, and rehabilitation exercises. On the mental side, there are preparation and goal-setting strategies, and mental rehearsal and focus techniques, to name a few. To become your best, you must take into account all the relevant components. In the next two chapters, we deal with physical conditioning.

Physical conditioning is critical for optimal table-tennis performance. Played at the highest level, the game is astonishingly fast and, though the rallies are generally short, it requires that you, as a participant, have a capacity for quick and powerful movements as well as sustained vigor and energy for play (which at some tournaments goes on for many days).

In addition to the obvious game-related benefits, regular physical activity can improve your health and physical well-being. For example, physical conditioning increases lean-body mass and nutritional efficiency, while reducing hypertension, pulse rate, and obesity. Physical conditioning also improves your mental well-being. It reduces anxiety and depression, and improves self-confidence, body image, self-concept, imaginativeness, emotional stability, and even intelligence.

What type of physical conditioning should you do to improve your game? We argue that those physical conditioning drills and exercises that use the actual movements of a sport are best for conditioning in that sport. The reason is relevance. These types of drills shape you in a way that is *directly applicable* to table-tennis play, while providing you with both aerobic and anaerobic conditioning. (Aerobic training is necessary because it enables you to sustain the rigors of prolonged activity during a tournament. Anaerobic conditioning gives you the explosive muscle speed that helps you to be balanced and in the proper position for each shot, along with the power to put balls away with smashes and loop kills.) Because these drills use the movements of actual play, the conditioning you get from them is readily transferable to actual play. Hence, looping, loop-killing, smashing, and quick-paced footwork drills are ideal for anaerobic conditioning. Activities such as stroking and slower-paced footwork drills, requiring less explosiveness, are excellent for improving aerobic capacity. Other conditioning drills, though important, are less useful because they give you a type of conditioning that is less transferable to table-tennis play.

In what follows we suggest drills—stroking, footwork, and service and service-return drills—designed to better your aerobic and anaerobic table-tennis performance as well as improve motor functioning. For each of the drills sketched below, the order of presentation corresponds to the degree of difficulty.

STROKING DRILLS

In this section, we illustrate some of the more common stroking drills and offer certain variations of these. Our list of drills is far from complete. For variety, draw from these and devise new drills that agree with your style of play. Creativity is the key here. Use enough diversity to eliminate boredom, but enough sameness to be capable of measuring improvement. In drills in which you and your training partner have distinct roles, switch roles after a sufficient amount of time.

Crosscourt Counterdrive Drill (and Options)

Whether done in the forehand-to-forehand or backhand-to-backhand fashion, this is the most popular stroking drill in today's game. The only problem? It is overdone. Players see professionals do this drill before a match as a means of warming up and they conclude that these professionals spend the bulk of their training time in crosscourt hitting. Try variations of this when practicing. For the forehand, hit down the line or hit forehands from the backhand end of the table (see figure 6.1). For the backhand, try alternating a backhand counter with a backhand corner stick, or counter one then step away from the table and backhand loop the next. From either the forehand or

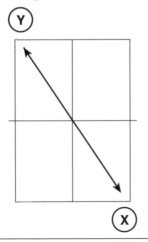

Figure 6.1 Forehand crosscourt counterdrive drill. Here X and Y exchange crosscourt forehands—concentrating on consistency, technique, and ball speed.

backhand corner, hit one hard, then one soft, forcing your partner to practice the front-and-back two-step footwork in conjunction with a consistent hit.

Crosscourt Push Drill (and Options)

These crosscourt drills are the standard ones for honing the push strokes (see figure 6.2). You may also practice down-the-line variations (forehand to backhand, backhand to forehand). Remember to use full strokes. This is an especially important drill if you are a beginner.

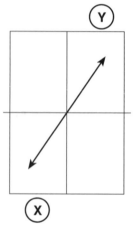

Figure 6.2   Backhand crosscourt push drill. Here X and Y exchange backhand pushes—perhaps focusing on varied depth and spin.

For variation, change the depth and amount of spin on each ball while maintaining consistency.

Loop to Block Drill (and Options)

The forehand version of this is essential for elite play and you should practice this drill extensively, being able to sustain many loop-block combinations in a row (see figure 6.3). We suggest that you practice the backhand version of this and be capable of sustaining a strong backhand loop against weaker topspin shots like a block or soft counter. Both of these stroking drills are simple, yet important for offensive-minded players.

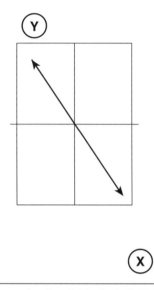

Figure 6.3 Forehand loop to forehand block drill. While X loops crosscourt, Y blocks in return.

For variety, you, as the looper, may vary the speed and spin of the loops, or your partner, the blocker, may vary the blocks, blocking one soft and short, then one hard and deep. Always try to build up the tempo during this drill by increasing the speed of your loops. As we say in chapter one, the speed of a loop against topspin is a more effective weapon than heavy spin. Also, when looping, vary your timing. Catch the ball on the rise, at the top, and on its descent. These timing variations will make your loop harder to defend by throwing off your opponent's timing.

Loop and Counter to Block and Counter Drill

Here you alternate one loop with one counter, crosscourt, while your partner alternates one block with one counter (see figure 6.4). Once the forehand loop and counter are properly mastered by themselves, this drill is an excellent way to learn to work both together. Failure to be mechanically fluid and sound at this drill means that you will be unable to switch from counters to loops (or the converse) in games or game-situation drills where counters and blocks are not so neatly placed. You must master this drill to be flexible and unpredictable from your forehand side.

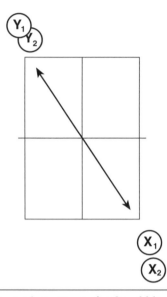

Figure 6.4   Forehand loop and counter to forehand block and counter drill. X alternates loops and counters, while Y alternates blocks and counters. Note that X's loop position, X_2, is deeper than his counter position, X_1, and that Y's block position, Y_2, is right at the table.

You may also practice this drill by using comparable backhand shots.

Forehand Loop to Forehand Loop Drill

This is a first-rate anaerobic conditioning drill popular with European players (see figure 6.5). The object is obvious: By practicing loop against a loop, you hope to develop a capacity for taking the offensive advantage away from your opponents. Stand high and try to graze the top of the ball with a closed racket, imparting some right-to-left sidespin (or left-to-right, if you are left-handed). Perform this drill crosscourt. The key here is consistency: Beginning with safe loops, build quickly to powerful drives. Do not expect to be able to execute more than five or six in a row at any level of play.

Topspin to Topspin and Chop Drill

While your partner alternates forehand chops and counters, you loop the underspin shot and counter the topspin shot with your forehand.

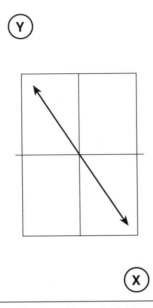

Figure 6.5   Forehand loop to forehand loop drill. Here both players exchange forehand loops while away from the table.

This drill, illustrated in figure 6.6, teaches you how to consistently alternate between countering topspin and looping chop, while your partner practices alternating chops and counters away from the table.

Practice this also by using backhands only.

Multiball

The feeder, your partner, with a box of balls placed on the table, feeds pushes with varied spin and height to you to one spot on the table. You proceed to either hit or loop these feeds in rapid-fire succession, varying your shot according to the amount of underspin on the ball.

This is an excellent anaerobic conditioning drill for building game-situation power, as well as a fine aerobic conditioning drill. To concentrate on anaerobic conditioning with this drill, have your partner feed the balls to you slowly, while you emphasize explosiveness and good form. A quickened pace that concentrates less on power and more on endurance will condition you more aerobically. For a change, have the feeder mix some topspin with the underspin, or, as hitter, alter your placement on the other end of the table.

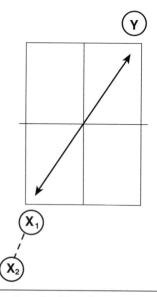

Figure 6.6 Backhand topspin to backhand topspin and chop drill. Here Y sustains a backhand topspin shot to X, who alternates a topspin, X_1, and a chop, X_2.

Multiball can be used to simulate any drill, and it functions much the same way as many of today's robots. The advantage of this drill is the natural variation that comes from the human hand. Robots always give you the same speed and spin and, as a player, you come to respond mechanically. In game play, you are constantly adjusting to your opponent's ball, which changes naturally from shot to shot. Our recommendation: Stay away from robots! Practice multiball.

We can mention plenty of other drills, but again space limits us. Use your imagination to think up varieties of these drills, tailored to your style of play.

FOOTWORK DRILLS

Good footwork increases your chances of being in set position to make a sound shot during match play. Because of the speed of the ball during play, often you have to prepare for a stroke while you are in transition from one end of the table to another. In certain cases, you do not have enough time to move into the correct position, let alone get ready to make a shot such as a backhand loop. You will frequently have to begin your shot while moving. Consequently, you need to practice sound footwork techniques, and the footwork drills we will mention are ideal. They allow you to effectively employ the stroking skills you have honed and condition you in a sport-specific manner.

Crosscourt and Down-the-Line Topspin Drill

Alternate a forehand counterdrive down the right side of the table with a backhand counterdrive down the left side, as shown in figure 6.7. Your partner responds by alternating forehand and backhand counterdrives crosscourt. In this drill, both of you get to practice controlled forehand and backhand stroking along with the lateral two-step drill. Going down the line is slightly more difficult and requires swifter footwork. As the level of mastery improves, increase the speed of the volleys, but not at the expense of correct footwork.

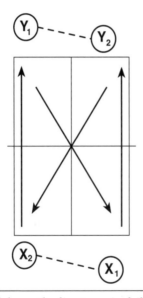

Figure 6.7 Crosscourt and down-the-line topspin drill. Here Y alternates between a crosscourt forehand counter, Y_1, and a crosscourt backhand counter, Y_2, while X alternates between a down-the-line forehand counter, X_1, and a down-the-line backhand counter, X_2.

Crosscourt and Down-the-Line Push Drill

This is the same drill as the crosscourt and down-the-line topspin drill except that pushes are used here and play will be closer to the table.

One-One Topspin Drill

Use the lateral two-step to play one wide forehand with topspin, then one middle forehand with topspin (see figure 6.8). Your partner will simply counter from either the forehand or the backhand side.

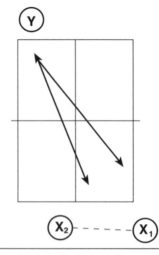

Figure 6.8 One-one topspin drill. As Y places a forehand counter, first deep to X's forehand side, X_1, then to the middle of the table, X_2, X plays a forehand counter from both positions.

In a sport where the forehand mostly controls play, this drill teaches you to handle balls just outside your forehand hitting zone. Balls inside the forehand hitting zone are easily handled, but balls placed to the left or right of the zone require sure footwork. This drill enables you to move wide to your forehand side and recover to protect your vulnerable middle with another forehand.

Two-One Topspin Drill

Have your partner, from the backhand end, counter two backhand topspins to your backhand corner, then one to your forehand corner. You, at your backhand end and hitting only to your partner's backhand, play a backhand, then a forehand from this side. Last, moving to your forehand side, play a forehand. After this, move again to your backhand court, and the cycle continues (see figure 6.9).

This drill teaches you how to play a forehand from your backhand side and how to recover to play a ball to your wide forehand.

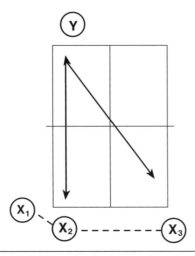

Figure 6.9 Two-one topspin drill. *Y* places two forehand counters to *X*'s backhand side, X_1 and X_2, then one to *X*'s forehand court, while *X* plays first a backhand counter, (X_1), second a forehand counter, (X_2), and last a forehand counter, (X_3).

In doing so, it gives you good footwork practice by combining the footwork of the backhand corner two-step drill with that of the crossover two-step drill. For variation, let your partner counter from the forehand side of the table.

Up-and-Back Two-Step Drill

Counter a crosscourt forehand from your forehand side of the table, move away from the table using proper footwork, then loop (or counter) from here. Your opponent plays a steady forehand counter. You should also practice a backhand version of this drill and the two down-the-line versions. Figure 6.10 illustrates the forehand version only.

This drill employs the front-and-back two-step footwork—giving you practice in moving to and from the table. Of the footwork drills, this is the most difficult, but one of the most important for accomplished play.

Random Topspin Drill

Once you have mastered specific footwork drills, the random topspin drill is an excellent way to work them into game-situation

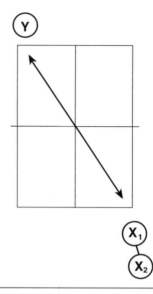

Figure 6.10 Forehand up-and-back two-step drill. Y alternates between a firm, steady counter and a hard counter to X who counters, first at the table, X_1, then away from the table, X_2.

practice. Here you send topspin balls, loops and counters to either your partner's backhand or forehand side of the table, while your opponent randomly counters balls crosscourt, to the middle, or down the line on your end of the table (see figure 6.11).

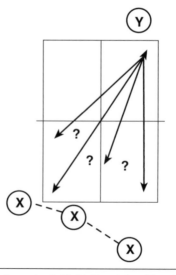

Figure 6.11 Random topspin drill. Y directs backhand topspin to all parts of X's table, while X places both forehand and backhand topspins to Y's backhand.

While hitting balls randomly to you, your opponent does not do so with the goal of beating you, but rather with the aim of challenging you to get to each ball using proper footwork and sound strokes. Therefore, your partner's placement and ball speed will be equal to your ability to use good form and footwork. As your ability improves, your partner can increase the speed of the topspin shots and vary the placement even more. To make this drill more difficult, you and your partner can topspin randomly.

The goal of this drill is steadiness (being on your toes and ready to move anywhere) and proper technique. It is a difficult drill to perform correctly; it requires mastery of the topspin stroking and footwork drills. It is also an effective practice tool because, unlike many of the drills you practice, this one simulates actual play.

Random Push Drill

Your opponent pushes to any part of the table, using a variety of underspin techniques, while you push to the forehand or backhand side, as shown in figure 6.12. As a more difficult variation of this, both you and your partner can push randomly. Because pushing is slower than countering, focus on correct footwork and precise stroking.

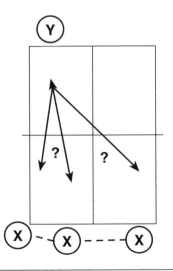

Figure 6.12 Random push drill. Here *Y* directs forehand pushes to all parts of *X*'s table, while *X* returns both forehand and backhand pushes to *Y*'s forehand.

SERVICE AND SERVICE-RETURN DRILLS

As we stress in chapter two, you must regularly practice both service and service return to improve your game. To better this facet of the game, you must be innovative and imitative, and you must experiment. Because most drills for service are also service-return drills, we deal with both together.

Single Service Drill

First, let us recommend a simple drill that you should use regularly, especially if you are a novice. Choose any serve and practice it while your partner attempts a certain response to that serve. Then, merely catch your opponent's return and begin again. Do not play out the point. Though this appears to be a simple drill, it is valuable. With concentrated practice, you as server will learn how to do a particular serve well and your partner will learn how to execute a specific response to that serve. If you have not mastered this drill (from both a service and service-return perspective) with a variety of serves, do not attempt to move on to more difficult types of service and service-return drills. To increase the difficulty of this drill, either play the point out or have the returner vary her responses to the same serve.

Single Service Look Drill

Having mastered this first drill, you may practice mixing specific kinds of one serve to give the same "look." For example, you may use any one of the serves that we have illustrated in chapter two and practice its different types. From the server's perspective, practice spin, speed, placement, and, most of all, deception. As a receiver, learn a quick read and choose the best response to each particular serve. Remember to vary your responses for unpredictability. Again, you may play out the point to increase the degree of difficulty.

Two-Two Service Drill

"Two-two" is a more complicated drill. Serve continuously until your partner wins two consecutive points. Now your partner becomes the server and you try to earn back the serve by winning two consecutive points. By cleverly mixing your serves, you can often keep your partner from serving for a few minutes or even more. The advantage of this drill is that it simulates game play without the tension of scorekeeping. In general, increase the frequency of this type of drill as a competition draws nearer.

Service Zone Drill

When no partner is available, you can practice serving alone as long as you have a bucket of balls. To give you a definite practice target, place six balls in six fixed positions in the service zones (chapter two) and try to knock them off the table. Do this either successively, not going to the next zone until you strike the ball from one zone, or randomly, trying for a different ball on each serve regardless of the outcome. This drill gives you excellent service-placement feedback. You should be able to knock off all six balls within 25 tries.

Play Without Serving Drill

When trying to improve your service return, play an 11-point game without the advantage of serving. Against a strong opponent with good serves, winning seven points or more is a good goal. Against a weaker player, try to be the first to 11.

Between these types of service and service-return drills, think up a variety of others. If you are a beginner, do simpler drills more often, such as the first drill mentioned, in which many restrictions are imposed on the serve and return situation. Also, concentrate on simpler service drills when a contest is still far away. Those in which few or no restrictions are imposed, like the two-two drill, are good just before a tournament or when you have mastered the simpler drills.

Chapter 7

Total Conditioning

The 1991 World Champion, Jorgen Persson of Sweden, pushes a serve back from his backhand end.

I n advanced-level training regimens, sport-specific conditioning is supplemented with conditioning of a more general sort. First and perhaps most importantly, sport-specific drills, when used as the exclusive means of conditioning, can get monotonous—bringing about poorer performance. Second, sport-specific drills do not always help athletes attain a *special* type of desirable conditioning. As a table-tennis player you can definitely improve power and overall strength by practicing certain table-tennis drills. However, you can improve strength and power more quickly and effectively by incorporating some weight lifting into a conditioning program.

When choosing nonsport-specific or auxiliary conditioning drills, be careful that the type of conditioning you choose is easily transferable to your table-tennis game. Therefore, the best type of auxiliary physical conditioning, though not sport-specific, most closely resembles the movements you use in table tennis or is executed so it improves table-tennis performance. By choosing relevant auxiliary exercises and performing them properly, you can be assured of developing a usable type of fitness.

In what follows, we suggest some supplemental aerobic and anaerobic conditioning drills and exercises.

TOTAL AEROBIC CONDITIONING

Aerobic activity occurs over a long time, from many minutes to a few hours or, in extreme cases, a few days. It is so named because it relies critically on the heart and blood to carry oxygen to the working areas.

Like any other means of improved conditioning, the goal of increased aerobic conditioning is to gradually increase the stress on your body's energy-producing ability—placing progressively more stress on the heart, lungs, blood vessels, and enzyme-producing capacity. In this way, over time, your body will improve its cardiovascular fitness and you will be better able to endure the rigors of serious table tennis.

As your aerobic fitness improves, exercise intensity—measured at one time or over time—must become greater or further fitness is impossible. Improved fitness comes by constantly recovering from and increasing the stress demands imposed on the body. However, as stress demands and bodily fitness increase, your body's ability to adapt to further stress is diminished. Plateaus become more frequent as you begin to reach the pinnacle of your ability, and more and improved means of rest become necessary. Consequently, as figure 7.1 shows, the road to sport elitism is pyramidal.

The preferred type of aerobic drills you perform should be, as we argue in the previous chapter, sport specific. For auxiliary and general aerobic conditioning, running, swimming, jumping rope, and even very light weight lifting with little or no rest between sets are

Figure 7.1 The pyramid of sport elitism. Improved play involves increased intensity and conditioning. Very few athletes make it to the highest level of performance, the elite level.

beneficial activities. Transferability, here, is not a problem because improved cardiovascular fitness is your main concern and all these activities will facilitate this. If, for instance, you choose running as your main aerobic means of auxiliary conditioning, push yourself to improve your running. To improve aerobic fitness while running, you must either lessen the time in which you complete the run or increase the distance while maintaining your rate of speed. For example, if you complete a 4-mile (roughly 6.45-kilometer) run in 28 minutes, set a conditioning goal of either averaging the same distance in 24 minutes or completing a 6-mile (9.7-kilometer) run in 36 minutes. In either case, you have certainly improved your aerobic conditioning.

What this means is that, to improve conditioning of any sort, you must constantly strive to break the "sameness barrier." You can expect no improved play if you constantly perform the same drills in the same manner with the same consistency for the same amount of time. Improved tournament play comes by means of improved conditioning in training sessions. For example, if you can only forehand loop to a sustained block for 5 minutes before fatigue sets in, strive to build up to 10 minutes. Likewise, improving the speed with which you perform the crosscourt and down-the-line topspin drill, as long as there is no diminution in the level of execution, is a sign of improved motor skills. By constantly breaking the sameness barrier, over time you will see substantial improvement in your game.

At some point, you may decide that a certain level of aerobic conditioning is suitable, because too great a focus on it may leave you with too little left for sport-specific conditioning. Here, then, strive to *maintain* a particular level of aerobic auxiliary conditioning while improving sport-specific conditioning. When you begin to plateau at sport-specific conditioning, you may decide to again focus chiefly on improving your previous level of aerobic conditioning.

TOTAL ANAEROBIC CONDITIONING

Anaerobic activities, activities not critically involving oxygen, are those that require quick, explosive strength and last from a few seconds to a few minutes in length. The muscular movements are so quick that they happen before the body can supply oxygen via the blood to the areas being worked. Examples of anaerobic activity are a sprint, a set of repetitions in a weight lifting exercise, and the forehand kill in table tennis.

As a table-tennis player you must condition yourself anaerobically to increase strength and power, improve flexibility and muscular coordination, reduce body fat, and, overall, build a more work-efficient body. As with aerobic training, the kind of anaerobic exercise we principally endorse is sport specific. In addition to some of the drills mentioned in chapter six, three- or five-ball-killing, loop-killing, and smashing (against a sustained lob) drills are the types of exercises that will develop power. You must keep in mind, however, that in the execution of such drills, there should be total focus on faultless performance and all-out effort when putting the ball away. There can be a few seconds rest between sets, for the chief goal here is not building wind, but power.

The type of supplemental anaerobic conditioning we encourage is strength training with weights. If done correctly, this is the most efficient way for the majority of athletes in all sports to improve anaerobic conditioning. Lifting weights is the most effective way to build muscle, and its metabolic benefits make it an excellent way to lose fat as well. Weightlifting will not slow you, nor will it make you muscle-bound or, if you are a woman, masculine looking. Done correctly, it will improve your speed of movement and muscle-to-body fat ratio, making you fitter.

In what follows we suggest and illustrate 11 weight lifting exercises that you can incorporate in your overall conditioning program. Do these in the order of presentation and exactly in the manner specified. As with table-tennis play, thoroughly stretch and warm up your muscles before you begin any lifting (see chapter five).

The Parallel Squat

With the barbell resting comfortably but high on the back of the shoulders, spread your feet about a foot wider than shoulder-width and point your toes slightly outward. With your back arched backward, descend very slowly until your upper legs are parallel to the floor. At this point, spring upward and accelerate, slowing just before completion. At completion, keep your body fully erect and lock your knees.

Throughout the lift, your back should not fall forward, but should remain rigid. Keep your knees pointed in the exact direction of your feet. They should not fall in toward each other, nor should they stick outside the line of the feet. Do three sets of 8 to 12 repetitions in a *progressive* fashion (e.g., 150 pounds x 12, 175 x 12, 200 x 12). This exercise strengthens the quadriceps, the buttocks, the hamstrings, the lower back, and the abdominals (see figures 7.2 and 7.3).

The Forward Lunge

Standing upright with your feet relatively close together and with a light dumbbell in each hand, lunge forward with the right leg until it is bent to a right angle, then thrust back to the upright position. Repeat this activity with the left leg. Three sets of 15 repetitions in *standard* fashion is sufficient (e.g., 10 pounds x 15, 10 x 15, 10 x 15). The lunge works most of the same muscles that you work in the squat, but in a slightly different manner. It is a great exercise to improve quickness to and away from the table.

The Bench Press

With the weight fully extended at arm's length, your back flat on the bench, and your arms about 30 inches apart, descend slowly

Figure 7.2   Parallel squat, part one.

Figure 7.3   Parallel squat, part two.

with the weight, in an arced fashion, to the chest. At the chest, accelerate up to completion so that someone, looking downward at the bar, would see it perpendicular to the body at the top. We recommend three sets in a progressive manner (e.g., 100 x 10, 125 x 10, 150 x 10). The pectorals, the triceps, and the front deltoids are chiefly used in the bench press.

Stiff-Legged Deadlift

Standing with a barbell directly in front of you and your feet shoulder-width apart, bend forward with a slight bend in the knees, grab the barbell, and lift until you are standing erect. Keep the bar close to your legs throughout. Lift the bar *slowly* and *smoothly* on the upward and downward parts of the lift (see figures 7.4 and 7.5). Do three sets in a progressive fashion (e.g., 75 x 15, 100 x 15, 125 x 15).

The stiff-legged deadlift works the hamstrings, lower back, trapezius, and upper back.

Figure 7.4 Stiff-legged deadlift, part one.

Figure 7.5   Stiff-legged deadlift, part two.

The One-Arm Bent-Over Row

With the left knee and hand resting on a bench for support and a moderately heavy weight in the right hand fully extended downward, pull the dumbbell upward quickly, then slowly take it back downward. On the upward pull, tuck your elbow in toward the upper back and pull the weight upward as far as the movement grants, allowing the upper back a full contraction. Perform three sets in a progressive fashion (e.g., 50 pounds x 10, 65 x 10, 80 x 10). This exercise works the whole upper back, the trapezius muscles, the biceps, and, to a lesser extent, the lower back.

The Abdominal Crunch

For this exercise, lay flat on the floor with the legs elevated against any wall. Holding a weight behind your head, bring your chest up and then inward, toward the abdominals. The abdominals will feel crunched together at contraction. Hold this position for a second, then repeat. We suggest three sets of 15 repetitions in standard fashion (e.g., 25 pounds x 15, 25 x 15, 25 x 15). Abdominal crunches isolate the stomach muscles.

The Standing Biceps Curl

Standing upright, with the legs about shoulder-width apart, curl the barbell quickly to the top of the chest, keeping the elbows as stationary as possible at the sides of the body throughout the lift. At the top, descend the barbell slowly to the starting position. The use of a curling bar is preferable to a straight bar because it puts less stress on the elbows.

We suggest three sets of 12 repetitions in standard fashion (e.g., 65 pounds x 12, 65 x 12, 65 x 12). (This exercise may be *supersetted* with the triceps extension, which follows immediately. To superset, upon completion of one set of 12 repetitions of the biceps curl, immediately do a set of triceps pushdowns. Because these exercises work antagonistic muscles, the curls will not greatly affect your ability to perform the pushdowns to follow. Rest from one and one-half to two minutes before performing the second superset.) The standing biceps curl, done properly by moving only the lower arm, will isolate the biceps muscles and the muscles of the lower arm.

The Triceps Extension

This exercise neatly isolates the triceps. While prone on a bench and using a barbell—beginning with the bar fully extended and with the elbows tucked to the sides of the body—gradually bring the bar down to your forehead by moving the lower part of the arm only, keeping your elbows motionless all the while. With your arms bent to roughly an 80-degree angle at the head, slowly bring the bar back upward to the beginning position by moving only your lower arm, again keeping your elbows motionless. This exercise isolates the muscles at the back of the arm. Do three sets of 12 repetitions in standard fashion (e.g., 50 pounds x 12, 50 x 12, 50 x 12).

The Side Bend

With the left hand by the left hip and a relatively heavy dumbbell in the right hand, lower the dumbbell downward to the right knee by expanding the muscles on the left side of the waist, the left obliques (see figures 7.6 and 7.7). This movement, a slow bending toward the side of the right knee, works the muscles on the left side of the body. Next, return to the starting position of standing straight up. We suggest 12 to 15 repetitions in standard fashion (e.g., 60 pounds x 15, 60 x 15, 60 x 15). This exercise strengthens the obliques, which stabilize the lower spine and help prevent lower-back injuries.

The Calf Raise

Holding a dumbbell in the left hand, rest the ball of the right foot on any steady, blocklike platform from four to six inches high, and hold onto any steady object with the right hand for balance. Bring the body downward, fully stretching the right calf muscle, then move the whole body upward by fully contracting this calf. Do the same for the left calf. Perform three sets of 15 repetitions in standard fashion (e.g., 50-pound dumbbell x 15, 50 x 15, 50 x 15).

Figure 7.6   Side bend, part one.

Figure 7.7   Side bend, part two.

Calf raises can be supersetted with wrist curls. Calf raises strengthen the calves, allowing greater and quicker mobility at the table, and help to stabilize the knee because part of the calf muscle extends beyond the knee.

The Wrist Curl

Hold a barbell while resting the lower arms on the end of a bench. Roll the barbell slowly downward to the end of the fingers, then quickly curl the bar upward using motion only at the wrists. Repeat this for 15 repetitions and three sets in standard fashion (e.g., 50 pounds x 15, 50 x 15, 50 x 15). This will strengthen your grip and the forearms.

For these exercises you need little rest between sets, no more than one and one-half to two minutes. Perform every exercise with absolute attention to detail and technique. On the final set of each exercise, do as many repetitions as you are capable of doing. Whenever you perform two sets of 12 repetitions in the triceps extension with 60 pounds and, on the third set, you get more than 12 repetitions, then use more weight, maybe 65 pounds, the next time. Again, never sacrifice technique for an additional repetition. The only measure for actual strength gain here is the ability to use more weight or do more repetitions in a particular exercise while doing the repetitions in a strict and consistent manner.

Concerning the speed of motion in the exercises, perform exercises 1 through 3, 5, 7, and 10 in a controlled fashion on the first part of the lift, but *explosively* on the second half of the lift. For example, for each repetition of the parallel squat, descend at a constant and slow rate, until you reach parallel, then explode upward to completion. Although this puts additional stress on the tendons and ligaments, the quick surge upward builds power (strength and speed) usable for table-tennis performance. Perform the other exercises—the stiff-legged deadlift, the abdominal crunch, the side bend, and the wrist curl—in a slow and controlled fashion in both the flexive and extensive parts of the lift.

Key Points

1. Choose auxiliary exercises that are relevant for and transferable to table-tennis play.
2. Strive to improve both aerobic and anaerobic conditioning.
3. Break the "sameness barrier" by striving to break performance training records.
4. Perform all exercises and drills with impeccable attention to detail.

Part III

COMPETING TO WIN

Jim Butler, one of the top players in the United States, backhand loops a deep push.

Chapter 8

Tournament Preparation

The 1992 Olympic bronze medalist, Kim Taek Soo, shown here completing a successful loop against moderate underspin at the 1995 World Team Cup.

There are many ingredients that go into the mix for successful table-tennis play. In this chapter we prepare you for tournament play by showing you what you can do before and during competition to enhance your performance.

PRACTICE SESSION EFFICIENCY

Most athletes in all sports feel that by putting in enough practice time their skills will improve. How many times have you heard, "Well, if I practiced *as long as* Waldner (1992 Olympic gold medalist), I'd be as good as Waldner"? This is not necessarily the case. In table tennis, as is true of all sports, more is not necessarily better. Though much practice time is essential for elite play, it is not sufficient to guarantee elite play. Many players devote many hours each week to practice with little or no results. It would be more sensible to say, "If I practiced as long as, *as intelligently as*, and *as hard as* Waldner, I'd be as good as Waldner." In this section we suggest some ways for you to improve your game by improving the quality of your practice sessions.

How do you make practice time pay off? The answer lies in efficiency. Put simply, you should train as intensely and intelligently as possible whenever you train. In training it is the quality of each session that counts, not the quantity of time put in or the gross number of training sessions per week. Fewer intense training sessions of short duration are more beneficial than longer and more frequent, though less intense sessions.

By their nature, intense sessions cannot last for hours and hours. Physiologically, your body wears down. Just as a car cannot run without gasoline or when it is in disrepair, your body cannot run without its fuel or when it is beaten down. When you train hard, lactic acid builds up in your muscles and your body's glycogen reserves become depleted. If you train hard for more than a few hours in any one session, your performance falls off and the time spent is not time well spent. Because of this, never let your practice sessions go beyond three hours. Two hours is ideal, with many short fluid breaks.

Another way to optimize practice-session efficiency is by having clear daily training goals. The best athletes in the world have daily practice goals, along with the determination and focus to attain them. Daily goals enhance focus, alleviate monotony, and are important for overall success.

Keep a strict log of all your training records, whether conditioning or skill records. If, in a particular training session, your focus is on footwork drills, pick a particular drill, like the two-one topspin drill, and try to perform it better than you have in the past. Aim to keep the ball in play for longer than you ever have without missing the table. Or, if the longest you have ever done this drill in the past has been 10 minutes, try to do the drill for 15 minutes with no lessening in the quality of performance. Whatever you do, try to break at least one conditioning or skill record every workout. These little daily "successes" will add up considerably, and the overall quality of your play, come tournament time, will be noticeably better. (For more on goal setting, see chapter 10.)

Key Points
1. Whenever you train, train with maximal intensity and focus.
2. Have clear daily performance goals.

CYCLE TRAINING

Cycle training is a means of varying your training to suit your conditioning needs. More and more athletes in all sports, from distance runners to weight lifters, are using this method. The benefits of cycle training are many, and undeniable. The main benefit is that it lets you, as an athlete, be in peak shape for your game when a table-tennis tournament arrives.

Regular intense training imposes extraordinary physical demands upon your body. In its turn, your body requires time for recovery—in extreme cases, up to 72 hours. From a weekly perspective, cycle training is a means of varying the physical intensity from training session to training session so your body may have sufficient recovery time and may not succumb to injury. From a monthly perspective, it helps you to develop an aerobic and anaerobic fitness base for an important tournament or period of competition in the future. Furthermore, cycle training is a planned way of breaking the "sameness" barrier. By writing out your sessions months in advance and establishing long-term training goals, you can plan weekly and even daily training goals designed to get you to your long-term goals. Moreover, cycling is also mentally beneficial because lack of workout variation leads to boredom and both lower intensity and focus in workouts.

In short, cycle training is a long-term method for varying the type, quantity, and intensity of your individual workouts to fit long-term goals. With respect to table tennis, it is best suited for either nonprofessionals who focus on fewer than a handful of competitions each year or professionals who want to be in peak shape for a large contest like the World Championships or the Olympics. Below, we suggest a sample cycle as an illustration.

Let us assume that you are a serious, nonprofessional table-tennis player who trains six days per week and has a full-time eight-to-five job. There are two major tournaments that you plan to attend this year, spaced four months apart, so devise a four-month cycle for each of these to be in peak condition for both contests. Now, break both cycles into three phases—a conditioning phase in which you emphasize generalized conditioning (30 percent of the cycle), a conditioning phase in which you concentrate on specialized conditioning (40 percent of the cycle), and a precompetitive phase (30 percent of the cycle)—so you arrive at five weeks for the first and last phases and seven weeks for the middle phase for each (see table 8.1). If you decide to train from Monday through Saturday, set up a one and one-half hour early morning session from Monday to Friday (perhaps from 5:30 to 7:00) and an early evening session (perhaps from 6:00 to 8:30). On Saturdays, go all out before your day of rest. Begin with an early morning two-hour session, then schedule an early afternoon two-hour session and an early evening one-hour session (optional).

Generalized Conditioning Phase

In the first phase, the generalized conditioning phase, focus mostly on honing good mechanics and developing an aerobic and anaerobic conditioning base to last up to the tournament. On Mondays, Wednesdays, and Fridays, spend your morning session lifting weights and using any remaining time working on problematic areas of your game. On Tuesdays, Thursdays, and Saturdays, begin the early session with a 4-mile or 6.45-kilometer run (or some other comparable aerobic activity like swimming), then spend the remainder of the time doing stroking and footwork drills. (Warming up should not count as part of a session.)

The early evening session, from Monday to Friday, may include two hours of stroking and footwork drills along with one-half hour of service and service-return drills. On Saturday, do footwork and stroking drills exclusively during the early afternoon session and

Table 8.1 Sample Cycle for Non-Professional Player

Generalized conditioning phase

	M	T	W	TH	F	S
Morning session	Lifting Problem areas	4 mile run Stroking Footwork	Lifting Problem areas	4 mile run Stroking Footwork	Lifting Problem areas	4 mile run Stroking Footwork
Evening session	Stroking Footwork Service Return	Stroking Footwork Service Return	Stroking Footwork Service Return	Stroking Footwork Service Return	Stroking Footwork Service Return	Stroking Footwork Service Return

Specialized conditioning phase

	M	T	W	TH	F	S
Morning session	Lifting Problem areas	4 mile run Stroking Footwork	Stroking Footwork	Lifting Problem areas	4 mile run Stroking Footwork	Stroking Footwork
Evening session	Service Return Game situation	Service Return Game situation	Service Return Game situation	Service Return Game situation	Service Return Game situation	Match play Problem areas

Precompetitive phase

	M	T	W	TH	F	S
Morning session	Lifting Problem areas	Stroking Footwork Service Return	4 mile run Stroking Footwork	Stroking Footwork Service Return	Stroking Footwork Problem areas	Match play
Evening session	Service Return Game situation	Match play	Service Return Game situation	Match play	Service Return Game situation	Match play Problem areas

devote the entire one-hour evening session working on service and return of service.

What is especially important here is that you establish distinct conditioning goals and set out to meet them by the last week of this phase. For instance, if you have been completing the 4-mile (6.45-kilometer) run in 32 minutes, strive to improve this time to 28 minutes or less.

Specialized Conditioning Phase

In the specialized conditioning phase, reduce your generalized conditioning and spend more time at the table. Lift weights only during your Monday and Thursday morning sessions, and run four miles only at the start of the Tuesday and Friday morning sessions. Perform stroking and footwork drills after each run and for the whole of the Wednesday and Saturday morning sessions. For the two and one-half hour early evening sessions on Monday through Friday, practice service, service-return, and game-situation drills. Set aside the two hours of the Saturday afternoon session for match play.

Figure 8.1 Danny Seemiller shows good form and concentration on the drive loop against light underspin.

On Saturday night, attack specific problems you have with your game.

In all, during this phase, you give more attention to improving specialized conditioning and game-simulating practice, while trying to maintain the generalized conditioning you achieved in the first phase. By the end of the seven weeks of the second phase, you will have met particular sport-specific conditioning goals—such as sustaining a record number of forehand loops against a steady block or improving the speed with which you execute the random topspin drill while maintaining consistency.

Precompetitive Phase

For the precompetitive phase, by limiting the generalized conditioning even further, you will have greater specificity of training than in phase two. The focus now is on game and game-situation play. Lift only at the start of your early morning Monday session and run only at the start of your Wednesday morning session. Perform stroking and footwork drills only during the Tuesday-through-Friday morning sessions. Do service and service-return drills Monday through Friday. Increase match play to four times a week—the Tuesday and Thursday evening sessions and the first two Saturday sessions. Address specific problems during the Monday and Friday sessions and Saturday evening. Practice game-situation drills during the Monday, Wednesday, and Friday evening sessions. While playing matches, do not focus too much on winning, but rather on utilizing appropriate game-situation techniques.

In general, this phase allows you to give absolute attention to impeccable technique on all your strokes, footwork drills, and practice combinations. In addition, keep strategies, opponents, and specific tournament goals foremost in your mind. Press yourself during training, but never so much that you have nothing in reserve. During match play, do not worry too much about winning and losing. Rather, meet technical goals during play. Play only select matches "all out" at specific times to give yourself some exact measure of your improvement and what you can expect at the tournament.

On the week of the competition, spend the last couple days resting from the rigors of your training cycle. Being so used to working hard each day, you may feel extraordinarily restless these final few days. Still, feeling restless at this time is a sign that you are in excellent physical and mental condition for the competition ahead and ready to perform robustly. At most, spend some, but not too much, time practicing serves. For the remaining time, rehash, reformulate, or revise playing strategies.

If you are a professional, you may have to vary such a routine greatly; the money offered by lesser tournaments on certain weekends, the need to give clinics, or the obligations of league play will remarkably alter or make impossible any well-prepared cycle. (We sketch a sample cycle for professionals in the Appendix.) If these commitments make cycling difficult or impossible for you, we suggest noncyclical variation—that is, varying the intensity of your training sessions during the week. In spite of these difficulties, we strongly advise that you cycle whenever you can—working clinics and weekend tournaments into your cycle, whenever possible. The benefits of well-planned cycling or, at least, varied training should be obvious, regardless of your level of play.

PROFESSIONAL INSTRUCTION

To reach the apex of your table-tennis potential, because the game is highly technical, you must learn all that you can about the game. There are different ways to do this. On one hand, no matter what your level of play is, read whatever you can that is relevant to your style of game. However, if you are an aspiring novice, before you start on your own, you need get some coaching or instruction. One excellent way to do this is by attending coaching clinics.

There are several clinics offered throughout the year by qualified professionals. Danny travels the U. S. giving clinics and instruction. Attending clinics by qualified coaches gives you early feedback on the basics of the game before bad habits become part of your game and limit progress. This will also give you some idea of the daily activities professionals pursue. We advise you to attend several clinics from different instructors. In this manner you will get a varied perspective on practice and play, and a broader table-tennis education.

Clinics also allow you interactive feedback. By reading an article on the forehand loop against underspin, you may understand it perfectly well, but fail to perform the loop in the manner specified, sometimes without even knowing this. At a clinic, a professional is there to demonstrate the loop stroke to you, and watch you perform the loop, correcting any mechanical flaws you have as they occur.

Moreover, you may question the instructor or offer your insights on aspects of the game for the instructor's comments.

Another fine means of learning about the game is video instruction. There are several excellent videos on the game offering insight on both fundamentals and advanced techniques. Again, sample from the best of these.

Also, tapes of world-caliber tournament play are often helpful. Watching the tactics and even mistakes of the game's finest players is a healthy supplement to video instruction. Though it is difficult to pick up subtleties in the serve by watching tapes in match play, it is an exceptional way to learn match strategy.

Perhaps the most efficient way of improving play is by having a qualified coach. In a study of the 1984 Olympics, most athletes who performed to their potential had programs, strategies, and problems worked out in consultation with a coach. The input of the coach created an atmosphere that seemed to give these athletes an important performance advantage. You, too, would likely derive the same benefits from a qualified coach.

The main problem in selecting a coach is competence. At every club there are several members who, at the drop of a hat, will willingly tell you everything you need to know about the game. Some will even instruct you whether you ask for it or not. Beware! These are usually mediocre players with outdated strategies or empty ideas. If the price is right, select a professional with a proven track record, yet one who will be capable of intelligent and sympathetic interaction. A coach should be sincerely interested in your improvement and capable of working with you through all the physical and mental elements of the game, even outside problems that may influence your play. Never hastily choose a coach; a competent one will ensure steady and rapid improvement.

Key Points

1. Attend different clinics by qualified coaches for interactive feedback.
2. Use video instruction.
3. Watch tapes of elite competitions.
4. Consider a qualified coach, especially if you are just starting.

FOOD AND FLUIDS FOR A COMPETITION

An integral part of competitive preparation is matching your food and fluid needs to the increased stress demands of competition. If you do not replace the fuel and water you use through intense exercise, ultimately your body will shut down. The only way you can avoid this situation in a competition is through *planned* rehydration and carbohydrate ingestion.

Eating for a Competition

Begin to increase your carbohydrate intake a few days before a tournament from the recommended 60 percent up to as high as 80 percent of your total caloric intake, with the extra carbohydrate calories coming mostly at the expense of fats. On the day of the tournament, three to four hours before competing, take in up to five grams of

Figure 8.2   Chen Ying Hua with the backhand loop against underspin.

carbohydrate for every kilogram (2.2 pounds) of your body weight. One hour before the tournament, take in a light carbohydrate meal: one or two grams per kilogram of body weight. Blood glycogen levels will peak approximately 15 to 30 minutes afterward and you will have ample reserves of fuel from which to draw. (Review chapter five for more information about carbohydrate ingestion.)

During a tournament ingest carbohydrates at approximately 30-minute intervals at a rate of up to 150 to 250 grams per hour, assuming you are playing almost constantly. (If not, reduce the rate about 30 percent.) At such a rate, your intake of carbohydrates will closely match blood-glycogen depletion, providing much needed energy and delaying fatigue. Take in these carbohydrates in small amounts throughout the day, not all at once.

Immediately after a tournament (or an intense practice session), you need to take in carbohydrates (and fluids) immediately. Because your body is now glycogen depleted, immediately drink about 400-calories worth (100 grams) of some fruit juice. This jolt of fructose will be quickly absorbed and will supply the fuel that helps to replace the glycogen that was once in the liver, muscle tissue, and blood. Next, consume complex carbohydrates. Only after carbohydrate ingestion is completed, take in about 30 grams of a high-quality protein.

While training for a tournament, eat up to seven small meals daily at even intervals to keep glycogen levels high and constant. This means a meal every three to four hours, even one in the middle of the night as we suggest in chapter five.

Fluid Intake for a Competition

Water is the single most important nutrient in your body. When you practice intensely, even if you are very fit, you may use over three liters of water in one hour. Loss of fluids affects your strength and speed of movement. As a serious athlete, you must take measures to ensure that you avoid dehydration during tournament play. During exercise, as we mentioned, your blood carries oxygen and glycogen to muscles and removes the lactic acid, which accumulates when muscle cells work. As body temperature rises, blood is also used for refrigeration purposes. Dehydrate the body ever so slightly and less blood is available for replenishing the muscles, waste removal, and refrigeration. Obviously, drinking after exercise is not enough; to prevent the negative effects of dehydration, you need to replace fluids before and during competitions.

For fluid replacement, water is generally adequate. Anything added to water thickens the liquid and makes absorption into the blood more difficult and lengthier. However, fructose-glucose drinks that are no more than 10 percent carbohydrate are ideal because they are thin enough to readily pass into the bloodstream and quickly provide your body with ready-to-use fuel.

In addition, exercise in hot environments can affect your performance even if you are well hydrated. You cannot expect peak performance in such conditions but, by taking in fluids, you can minimize the ill effects of the heat and perform closer to your peak than those who are unprepared. While in a tournament, match your fluid intake to the environmental conditions. If the conditions are extraordinarily hot and humid, increase your fluid intake significantly. In this way you can reduce the harmful performance effects of dehydration. This, in itself, will give you an important advantage over the vast majority of players who take fluid replacement lightly.

After playing, if you replace fluids quickly, you recover quickly. Here, let water be your preferred choice of fluid. After you take in three to five glasses of water, then turn to replacing glycogen with carbohydrate sources: first simple or high-glycemic sugars, then complex ones.

Key Points

1. A few days before a competition, keep carbohydrate intake high, up to 80 percent of total calories.

2. On the day of a competition, consume fluids before play. Three to four hours before, take in five grams of carbohydrate per kilogram of body weight. One hour before play, take in one to two grams of carbohydrate per kilogram of body weight.

3. During a competition, drink copiously, matching fluid intake to the temperature of the environment. Take in 150 to 250 grams of carbohydrate per hour, if playing relatively constantly; if not, take in 105 to 175 grams per hour.

4. After a competition, rehydrate with three to five glasses of water, then take in 100 grams of simple carbohydrate, followed by complex carbohydrates, then about 30 grams of protein.

Chapter 9

Tournament Tactics

France's Jean-Philippe Gatien preparing for a forehand from deep within his backhand end.

I n this chapter we discuss ideas and psychological techniques useful during match play. In the first section we suggest ideas for improved play. Next, we put forth strategies for use against all opponents. Third, we examine strategies against specific types of opponents. In the final section, we discuss practical psychological techniques.

IMPROVING YOUR PLAY

Young table-tennis players today want to play a power game. They devote countless hours of practice time to hitting and looping drills, and see every return as an opportunity for a strong opener. In doing so they ignore important elements of the game. In this section we look at three such elements: ball placement, the short game, and varying the spin.

Ball Placement

Ball placement is a part of elite play that nonelite players generally overlook. However, this facet of the game is more important than the speed or spin you impart on the ball. Many offensive-minded up-and-coming players who are in a position for a strong offensive shot, like a forehand loop, err in looping hard to an opponent's forehand or backhand alley, when a less forceful shot either to the middle of the table or very wide to a particular side would be more effective.

Never think that the only real way to win a point is to overpower an opponent. If you do, you will wind up forcing the attack, looking for opportunities that do not exist. Being able to keep opponents off balance by pinpoint placement sets you up for power shots like smashes and loop kills. As a thinking player you must make use of the *whole* table.

The first rule of ball placement is to stay away from opponents' power zones. Power zones are those areas of the table where players can make strong forehand and backhand shots with little or no movement. Like the ready position, power zones are not fixed but vary with respect to their position between shots. To illustrate, let us consider X and his opponent Y. During a short exchange, X and Y find themselves positioned as figure 9.1 shows, with X preparing to play a forehand counter and Y ready to receive. X readies himself so he will contact the ball approximately at point C. Now, Y's backhand power zone is roughly that area from her left hip, point B_1, to two feet to the left of this point, point B_2, or that part of her end defined by angle B_1CB_2. Her forehand power zone begins about one foot out from her right hip, point F_1, and extends three feet outward to point F_2. This zone is defined by that part of the angle F_1CF_2 that covers Y's end of the table.

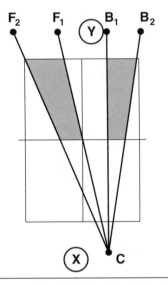

Figure 9.1   The power zones. The shaded parts of Y's end define that area where X does *not* want to place his shot. These are Y's power zones and, by placing a shot in one, Y will likely come back with an explosive, perhaps point-winning shot.

By placing balls into opponents' power zones you enable them to get off clean and powerful shots with minimal effort. More conservative shots placed to less safe parts of the table will prove a sounder strategy, resulting in many more points for you.

By elimination, by knowing where *not* to land the ball, you also know where to place it. The second rule, therefore, is place balls outside opponents' power zones. Wide placements force them outside the power zones. Because these shots require considerable footwork, they make it difficult for opponents to get into the ready position and stroke the ball crisply. Even if opponents happen to make a sure shot, it will be difficult for them to get back to a balanced position to make their next shot. In short, playing wide keeps opponents off balance, giving you a decided advantage during a match. Referring to figure 9.1, widely placed balls are those that would land on Y's end of the table, outside her power zones.

Last, playing to the middle, whether attacking or defending, is the most effective zone. This forces opponents to decide quickly between a backhand or a forehand. Often, they become hesitant or confused, if only for a split second, but this is enough to keep them from moving quickly to make a sure shot. On figure 9.1, shots to the middle would land within the angle F_1CB_1, just inside Y's power zones. Though such placements are conservative compared to very wide ones, they are effective when mixed with wide shots and are *always* preferable to playing directly to opponents' forehand or backhand power alleys.

As an additional element, many world-class players practice deceptive shots. For example, they may begin their shot as if they were going to stroke the ball to an opponent's forehand and then, at the last moment, direct the ball to the backhand side by a misleading turn of the wrist. Such shots are mechanically difficult, but quite effective because of their unconventionality. Because the catalog of such deceptive shots is virtually limitless, we shall not describe any of them here.

If you have a unique shot or two that have proven effective through the years, stay with them, but *do not overuse them*. First, because such shots are not technically correct and usually involve the wrist, they cannot be used effectively against all strokes. By using such shots indiscriminately, they lose their potency and consistency. Second, overuse lessens the surprise factor.

The Short Game

As players improve, they invariably notice they have more difficulty initiating the attack. This is because, at the lower levels of table tennis, short-net play is mostly nonexistent, whereas it is an indispensable tactic at the upper levels. Better players serve short most of the time and return short serves with returns that are also close to the net, thereby making the attack more difficult.

Playing close to the net requires finesse and a fine touch. These are not skills you are simply born with, but skills that you must hone by diligent practice, just like any others. Short serves and drop shots make it difficult for opponents to attack because, first, the table gets in the way of their swing when they move up to the ball and, second, there is little room for error against short (and especially spinny) shots.

For short service, serve the ball so it barely crosses the net and is able to bounce twice on your opponent's side when not returned, the last bounce touching as near as possible to the table's end.

Aggressive players will be tempted to loop the return, but will be unable to do so because the ball will just fail to clear the end of the table. In general, good short serves, especially those with a great deal of underspin, make it next to impossible for receivers to top-spin a return.

Practice short returns with a light touch. As with short serves, the goal is the same. You want to keep your opponents from attacking. Therefore, try to place the second bounce as near to the end of the table as possible.

A great short-game strategy, the drop shot (described fully in chapter one), is designed to draw in defensive-minded opponents who are away from the table and, ultimately, force an error. It is an integral part of elite play that should be practiced more at nonelite levels.

Varying the Spin

Varying the spin on the topspin strokes is a tactic Swedish players are using often for great effect, a tactic that has helped to slow the Chinese hitters' dominance of the game in recent years. Nevertheless, a wonderful example of someone who is able to vary the spin of his loops is the former Chinese player and current number one

Figure 9.2   England's Matthew Syed with a backhand chop.

player in North America (1995), Cheng Ying Hua. From what looks like the same loop stroke, by varying the amount of wrist he uses, often Hua spins the ball prodigiously, and at other times he only imparts a small amount of spin on the ball. Because opponents cannot read the spin of his deceptive stroke, they must wait on the ball before they return it. So, it is next to impossible to play these shots aggressively. By mixing the spin during your attack and varying the amount of wrist you use at contact, your opponents will have more difficulty reading your shots, forcing them to play cautiously.

When playing against opponents who use spin well, you must play alertly. If you cannot read the spin surely, wait longer before making your return. The longer the wait, the easier it will be to read the spin and respond accordingly. The drawback is that your opponents will have more time to ready for your return and prepare an effective shot. However, this drawback is outweighed by the gain: By not getting a good read, your opponents will assuredly gain the advantage. If you do not lose the point outright by stroking the ball into the net or over the table, your opponents will put away your ineffective return.

Against underspin serves and shots, use both heavy topspin and heavy underspin for varied effect. When pushing against underspin, vary heavy, light, and no-spin pushes and move these around the table.

Key Points

1. Ball placement is every bit as important as ball speed.
2. Stay away from opponents' power zones; play outside of these and toward the middle.
3. Be proficient at short-net play; as you improve, you will see more and more of this.
4. Vary the type and degree of spin shots.

STRATEGIES AGAINST ALL OPPONENTS

Against all opponents, you want to use your strengths and exploit their weaknesses. This obviously entails knowing something about their style of play. When preparing for players you have never faced and about whom you know nothing, you can learn much by watching them play. When scouting opponents, watch them serve and return serves. Noticing what serves they have, ask yourself what you will do when they give you a certain serve. Anticipate the types of returns they will have to your serves. Observe their overall style of play. Are they aggressive loopers or defensive strategists?

When you have carefully gleaned all the information available to you, develop a strategy that best agrees with your strengths and takes advantage of opponents' weaknesses. If the plan is sound, stick with it even if it fails to pay early dividends. For example, you may notice that a certain looper eats up blockers and choppers but has difficulty with other aggressive players. With a strong looping game yourself, you plan to win by beating this opponent to the attack. If you find yourself down 11 to 4 after a particular opponent's serves, it may not be that your plan is faulty. Perhaps you are not properly executing it. Maybe you are not aggressive enough against this opponent's serves. If, however, you are getting soundly defeated and there is good reason to believe that you are acting exactly according to plan, adjust it before it is too late, preferably in consultation with a coach or informed friend.

Remember and test for the following few general points before playing anyone.

First, *if opponents have a strong forehand, their backhand is probably weak.* You can test for this by hitting, looping, and pushing into their backhand during the warm-up or early in the match, or by watching them play another opponent.

Conversely, *when opponents have a strong backhand, their forehand is likely ineffective.* The same tests used for the backhand apply here.

Third, *if opponents counterdrive well, then their loop and spin game is probably weak.* Watch how such players react to heavy underspin and full topspin shots. Develop your strategy accordingly.

Fourth, *if opponents have a strong overall attack, their defense may be weak.* The way to test for this is by initiating a strong attack.

Fifth, *opponents with a strong defensive posture likely cannot attack well.* By adopting more of a defensive posture against such players, you force them to attack at least some of the time, more than they feel comfortable doing.

Last, *if opponents have poor footwork, it is likely that they are weak outside of their forehand and backhand power zones.* Exploit poor footwork by making such opponents cover the whole table: move them short and deep, left and right, and play some right at them.

Key Points

1. Gain all the information you can about an opponent before you play.
2. Devise a strategy before play, using some guidelines outlined earlier (and in the section immediately following), and stick to it.

STRATEGIES AGAINST SPECIFIC STYLES OF PLAY

Often before a match, because many players have a particular style of play, you will be able to categorize or label an opponent as a chopper, counterer, or blocker, for instance. In this section we give some tips for playing against specific styles of play.

How to Play Choppers

Against a defensive player, if you can overpower the defense, do so. For a power game, your main tools are the loop, the drop shot or short push, and, most importantly, the smash. Alternate short, spinny loops with deep, hard loops. Mix in a drop shot occasionally and, when the chopper puts the ball high, try to put the point away with a smash. If you lack the firepower of an aggressive game, use a more cautious and patient approach. Here are some general tips for mastering choppers' defense.

First, *know in advance the racket surface of each defender and have a plan for that surface.* The long-pipped and antispin surfaces are the most difficult to approach. We have more to say concerning these surfaces later.

Second, and most importantly, *be patient.* Choppers, by their style of play, are counting on you to become impatient. The defensive style is a game of attrition. Impatience always gives choppers the edge.

Next, *pay special attention to the spin of their shot.* Choppers are often excellent at varying the amount of underspin on their returns. No spin, light underspin, and heavy underspin are the three most likely types of spin you will get. Look for any visual clues that may help you read the spin, such as where choppers strike the ball on their bat, the amount of wrist used in the chop, and so forth.

Fourth, *attack the middle.* As with most players, choppers have more difficulty with balls played directly at them than with balls either to their immediate right or left, especially when they are close to the table. Balls directed right at them force them to make a quick decision whether to play a forehand or a backhand, and the result is a shot that is often less spinny and one that can be put away. Smashes and loop drives consistently score when directed at the chopper.

Fifth, *move choppers in and out, not side to side.* Playing into choppers' "wings" amounts to playing into their strength. Instead, drive choppers deep with hits and loop drives and pull them in with short, spinny loops and drop shots. Play to the sides occasionally for variation, but direct the attack right at them.

Sixth, *make frequent use of drop shots and pushes.* The push and drop shot are very effective against choppers when you combine them with more aggressive shots. Drop shots are most effective toward the forehand side of choppers. Most choppers can handle such shots more easily when placed to their backhand. When given to their forehand, the table often gets in their way and prevents good foot placement and a good shot, often forcing mistakes. Likewise, you must have a steady underspin push. Pushes, though less likely to force errors than drop shots, bring choppers up to the table and, over the course of a match, wear them out—adding variety to your attack.

Seventh, *let the depth and height of choppers' returns dictate the aggressiveness of your attack.* When the ball comes back short (near the net) or high, you must smash or attack the ball hard. The flat smash is indispensable against choppers for it generally wins the point outright. It is difficult to beat them without such a potent weapon. Against deep or low returns, be more conservative and try to set up a winner by a push or a spinny loop. A smash or loop kill against a low and heavily spun chop is not a high percentage shot. Choppers are counting on you to attempt and miss many such shots. You cannot miss these shots if you do not attempt them. Take what they give you—no more, no less. You are counting on their mistakes as much as they are counting on yours.

Eighth, *recognize traps.* Most defensive players have two or three patterns by which they trap you into overshooting. If you make two or three power shots and these are returned, change to a push to break the pattern. As an aggressive player, *you* should direct the pattern and tempo of attack by varying the type and amount of spin, and ball placement. Defensive players' style should be more reactive than active if the attacker is creative and designing. Choppers should never dictate the rhythm of the flow of volleys.

Last, *neutralize choppers' attacks*. An effective weapon for many choppers is their pick or hit. Seldom do they opt for more than one at a time. If you can consistently return this, you have gained an advantage and rendered their attack fruitless. In this manner, you prove to the defender that you too can defend and, more often than not, they will become defensive minded exclusively, and much easier to beat.

How to Play Loopers

Because of their aggressive style of play, loopers can be very difficult to play. Loopers who are consistent in their attack are even more unsparing and frustrating. The surest way to beat such players is to take them off their game. Against them, you must use aggressiveness to beat aggressiveness.

When playing loopers, *initiate the offense*. Serve short, then attack on the third ball. You need not begin a violent attack, just concentrate on beginning the attack. This puts loopers on the defensive, and loopers are usually weak when playing defensively.

Next, *do not push too often against loopers*. This is the shot against which loopers are most comfortable. When pushing, push either short or decisively deep into the corners. Short balls are hard to attack and balls pushed deep into the corners, when looped, leave the other corner of the table opened for a sharp block.

When forced to block, *do not block too passively*. Soft blocks aimed at the power lanes to the left and right of the loopers' table allow them ample time to set up for another aggressive loop. This enables loopers to establish a rhythm, and loopers in their rhythm are awfully tough to defeat. Challenge loopers with power blocks deep into the corners or directly at them. It is a good gambit, even if you miss. When you do not miss such blocks, you establish an aggressive (yet defensive) posture that keeps loopers uncertain of their ability to penetrate your defense.

Last, *play frequently to loopers' middle*. Loopers are generally strong on the wings but weak down the middle. Attack their middle often and aggressively with strong blocks and counters.

How to Play Penholders

As we mention in chapter one, due to their grip, penholders generally have strong forehands but weak backhands. Many penholders play up to 80 percent of their shots with their forehand. Because of this, to defeat penholders, there is only one rule: *exploit their backhand*. This is not as easy as it may seem. Most penholders display exceptional footwork and can cover a large percentage of the table with their forehand. To exploit their backhand, you must move the ball around. For instance, try playing a ball very wide to the forehand, then coming wide into the backhand corner. After a few times, when they come to expect the ball wide to the forehand, come to the backhand first. This compels even quick-footed penholders to use their backhand. In short, play them wide, but be unpredictable.

Whatever strategy you adopt, one that forces penholders to play their backhands will lessen the aggressiveness of their attack. To do this, you will have to play some balls deep and wide to their forehand before coming into their backhand. If you can get them to predictably play a weak backhand, this will enable you to play more assertively by using more of your power shots.

How to Play Blockers

Blockers are similar to choppers in that their style is defensive. Blockers are patient volleyers who work diligently and purposefully to move you out of position to win points outright or force errors.

Against blockers, *do not let them establish a rhythm*. Change your pace constantly. Loop one hard and deep, then counter, then loop soft and high over the net. High and spinny loops are preferable to hard ones because blockers are counting on forcing you out of position. Slow, spinny loops allow you to position yourself properly for the next shot.

Second, *try only one power shot at a time*. If a blocker returns this shot, then play the next ball safely. Blockers feed off consecutive attacks. Come back with a power shot when you are ready.

Third, as with the chopper, *be patient*. Blockers are usually poor at initiating an attack. Like the chopper, they rely heavily on your impatience. Make sound choices concerning which balls and when to attack. Your patience will be rewarded.

Last, *force or trick blockers to initiate the attack some of the time.* Blockers are most comfortable when you attack first. In fact, it is probably because they are so bad at initiating the attack that they have adopted a defensive posture. By making them attack sometimes, you force them to expose their weakness. You, then, gain the advantage.

How to Play Counterdrivers

Counterdrivers are very skillful playing both forehand and backhand counterdrives and usually play each the same percentage of time. In the main, they have poor footwork and are weak loopers, incapable of stringing together a series of loops during a given point. Here are a few things to keep in mind when playing the counterdriver.

First *avoid topspin rallies.* If you enter into too many rallies of this kind, you will be playing into their strength and will lose the lion's share of such encounters.

Second, *use underspin whenever possible.* This will slow down the rallies and take counterdrivers away from the topspin-hitting game with which they are so comfortable. When close to the table make good use of your pushes. In addition, do not be afraid to throw in a chop during a topspin rally. This will slow the pace and may force the counterdriver to hastily look for a way to reestablish topspin.

Working the middle of counterdrivers often is another key to defeating them. Because these players are mostly slow-of-foot, it is relatively easy to jam them with a shot to the middle.

Last, *use heavy spin.* Whether topspinning or underspinning the ball, counterdrivers are most relaxed with light spin. Lightly spun topspin balls are easily countered and lightly spun underspin balls may be easily hit or picked. By using a full array of spin shots you keep them occupied with your spin and away from their counterdrive game. This will slow their pace and force them into errors.

How to Play "Junk Rubbers"

Playing opponents with junk rubbers (e.g., long pips or antispin) may have already caused you more than a few headaches. What is typically frustrating about such rubbers is the apparent unpredictability in judging the type and amount of spin the ball has on any return of a given shot.

However, such rubbers really act predictably. Consequently, "junk rubbers" is a misnomer. The difficulty comes not in the unpredictability of such rubbers, but in many players not being able to fully understand how such rubbers work. For instance, when opponents with antispin block a spinny loop, the ball comes back with heavy underspin. This seems puzzling only because the same return with conventional rubber would yield a topspin return. In short, it is not that such rubbers behave strangely and unpredictably, but rather that players are unaccustomed to playing against them. Therefore, "unconventional rubbers" is the name we shall use hereafter.

In what follows, we give some pointers for playing against long-pipped rubber. When playing against antispin rubber, the same principles apply but to a lesser degree. To apply these principles to combination-racketed opponents (players with unconventional rubber only on one side) you must first remember which side of their bat has the unconventional rubber. You can easily do this by noting the color.

Opposite shots have opposite spins. When the long-pipped player chops your counterdrive, the ball will return with underspin. When such a player counters your push, you can expect topspin. This is no different than conventional rubbers.

Similar shots have opposite spins. If the long-pipped player counters one of your counterdrives, you can expect the opposite spin, underspin. If your push is pushed back with long pips, then you will receive topspin. In short, whatever spin you impart on the ball will be returned with the opposite spin regardless of what the long-pipped player does. The spin you receive is dictated by the spin you impart on the ball. (The only qualification here is the *amount* of opposite spin received in each of the two cases. In the case of opposite shots the amount of opposite spin received will be slightly greater than the amount of opposite spin received with similar shots.)

Long pimples cannot produce much spin on their own. What might look like a deep topspin serve may have slight topspin or even slight underspin on it. The same goes for what looks like a heavy undercut serve.

Lightly spun loops and pushes are very effective against long pimples. Lightly spun balls will be difficult to handle because unconventionally rubbered players cannot do much with these. Being unable to impart much spin on such balls, they will have difficulty controlling their returns and will generally not try aggressive shots. Consequently, those that are returned can be more readily attacked.

Remember, to master unconventional rubbers, you need to practically apply what you have learned about playing against such rubbers. The only way to do this is by playing frequently against them, because what you know from playing against conventional rubbers does not apply. By getting sufficient practice against unconventional rubbers, you learn that these rubbers have a logic to them and that there are general strategies you can use to overcome the perceived advantage unconventionally rubbered players have.

MENTAL TECHNIQUES

Just as table tennis requires much physical preparation, it also demands a considerable amount of mental preparation, or mental conditioning. Mental attitudes of accomplished athletes in all sports are causes of their athletic success. Elite athletes know how to deal with adversity and anxiety, how to stay mentally focused and alert, and how to solve problems that occur during competitions.

Following, we list some important mental techniques and suggest ways that you may use these to improve your play.

Mental Rehearsal

One mental skill that all elite athletes use to some extent is mental rehearsal. Mental rehearsal is the mental representation of an event to bring about a certain level of future athletic performance. For example, if you should wish to defeat a certain chopper in an upcoming match, you would imagine yourself beforehand successfully attacking her best deep topspin serve, third-balling your own serves, and so on.

As a table-tennis player you might use mental rehearsal to improve some aspect of your game, improve your overall game, maintain a certain level of performance, give yourself a feel for a competitive environment, or condition yourself for a good practice or competition. When it is done well, mental rehearsal seems true to the event for which it is being rehearsed.

According to some researchers there are two primary attributes of images in mental rehearsal: vividness and controllability. Vividness refers to the distinctness and clarity of the image in the mind. Controllability is the extent to which the image can be manipulated.

To become a good imager, you must be capable of bringing about a desirable, vivid image and manipulating that image.

Mental rehearsal is usually practiced in one of two ways: internally or externally. Internal imaging involves mentally performing the skill just like you are seeing and feeling the action from your eyes, as if you are actually performing the action. In contrast, external imagery is chiefly visual. Here you visualize yourself from outside your body performing to some desired level.

In imagery rehearsal, you practice by thinking through an initial mental representation that you hope will transfer to a future behavior, like your table-tennis performance. The key to a successful transference is the similarity of the two situations. The more you know about the future situation and the more realistically you practice rehearsal, the easier it is to transfer your images successfully.

Of late there has been great debate among psychologists concerning the benefits of imagery techniques. Many studies have conflicting data; other studies state causal connections that may not exist. Despite these uncertainties, there are some relatively uncontroversial findings that we summarize as follows.

First, almost all elite athletes use some sort of imagery training. One study reports that, at one Olympic Games, 99 percent of all Olympic athletes used some mental imagery as a preparation strategy. These athletes mentally rehearsed on the average four times per week for 12 minutes per session. Some athletes rehearsed for up to three hours in the last few hours of competition.

Second, mental rehearsal is more beneficial when you combine it with physical practice. Mental practice without physical training is of limited help in sustaining or improving upon a certain level of performance. For instance, there is no reason to believe that while injured you can maintain a certain level of table-tennis play through imagery alone.

Third, imagery is more effective for closed skills than for open skills. Closed skills are simple mechanical skills over which you have much control. An example is the golf swing or the table-tennis serve. Open skills are more complex, and external factors come to bear more significantly. An example is a table-tennis rally. Because most table-tennis skills are open, imagery techniques may be of limited value for the sport.

Fourth, the most effective and transferable images are those that are multisensory and not just visual. In other words, the greater the number of senses that you bring into mental rehearsal, the more the results will transfer. When imagining yourself performing a sustained forehand counterdrive, see and feel the bat strike the ball, hear the sound the ball makes when you strike it crisply and cleanly, and feel the appropriate muscles tense then relax. Even smell the air, musty from the sweat.

Fifth, the duration of the physical practice that follows the mental practice is important. Imagery is more effective for events that are at least one minute and no longer than five minutes. It becomes increasingly difficult to transfer imagery to events that are longer than this. Again, this sets limits to what you can effectively do with mental rehearsal for table tennis.

Last, the type of sport situation for which you are rehearsing determines whether you should use an internal or external perspective. You can best learn physical and motor-learning skills through an internal (first-person) perspective, especially if it is a closed skill. Timing skills are best learned through an external (third-person) perspective. Overall, an internal perspective is better for transferring imagery.

Mental rehearsal aids in performing certain athletic skills by narrowing and focusing attention. There may be limited benefits of mental rehearsal for table-tennis players because table tennis is mostly an open skill and, therefore, is not easy to visualize clearly and transfer.

In spite of its limitations for table-tennis play, we suggest that you use mental rehearsal where you can: for preparing your serves, for setting a mood at the table, and even for practice drills that are mostly mechanical, like stroking and footwork drills. For other aspects of the game, like service return and volleys, use it sparingly or not at all.

Now we lay out a few guidelines that may be helpful for learning to be a successful imager:

1. *Practice imagery techniques.* Just as it takes time to learn an effective backhand loop, it takes time to be an effective imager.

2. *Keep negative and irrelevant thoughts completely out of your head while imaging.* Negative thinking, by disrupting your focus on the task ahead, leads to poor performance.

3. *Determine your correct level of arousal when rehearsing.* Too great a level may result in a needless expenditure of energy and high performance anxiety; too little arousal is usually a sign of poor mental focus. Either extreme usually results in poor future execution.

4. *Rehearse only for those things over which you have some control.* Imagining that all your opponents in a tournament will play subpar is absurd because this is something over which you have little control (and something that is grossly improbable!). Imagining that you yourself are hitting crisp volleys and, overall, playing better than usual is not.

5. *Do not use imagery techniques as an exclusive means of practice.* Use mental rehearsal along with physical practice.

6. *Bring in as many senses as you can while rehearsing.* In rehearsing a serve, see yourself serving internally, feel the bat strike the ball, hear the ball hit the table twice, and so forth.

Figure 9.3 Cheng Ying Hua shows successful execution of the loop against heavy underspin. His feet leave the ground as he thrusts his way upward. The follow through is straight up, enabling him to overcome the heavy underspin.

Arousal

Table-tennis players have their own style, their own character. Some get very psyched, charging around aggressively after every point they win. With such an outward display, there can be no question of their focus and commitment to winning. Others—seemingly unemotional, silent, and unassuming—appear to play with a calm confidence, though somewhat less aroused. Both types are focused, but do the highly aroused players have any advantage over their quietly confident opponents? Or, is highly aroused play itself a disadvantage?

Arousal is a measure of physical and mental intensity or energy. Physically, arousal is characterized by increases in heart rate, blood pressure, blood sugar, and sweating, to name a few. In contrast, narrowed attention, fatigue, depression, dizziness, confusion, and loss of control are mental signs of arousal. Although too little arousal is obviously detrimental (a sure sign of lack of motivation), the physical and mental signs of arousal themselves suggest too much arousal can be bad as well. What is the right level of arousal for optimizing table-tennis performance? The question does not have an easy answer.

The precise relationship between arousal and performance is not fully understood. However, this much is understood: Different athletic tasks demand different levels of arousal. "Psyching-up" has been shown very beneficial for closed skills (for which the environment is relatively stable) and tasks requiring great muscular coordination, strength, speed, and endurance, but less beneficial and sometimes even harmful for open skills (for which the environment is constantly changing). Because the skills involved in table tennis are mostly open, they are less friendly to heightened arousal than, say, hurling the javelin.

Because table tennis is a complex and speedy game, temper your emotions by common sense. Too little arousal is a sign that your head is not sufficiently in the game. Too much may lead to overly aggressive play, a tendency to be easily distracted, and inability to think on your feet. Being a table-tennis enthusiast, you probably have no need to worry about being underaroused. Merely be wary of overarousal. Shouting and loud displays of emotion may sometimes seem unavoidable but, as a rule, such behavior detracts from your focus and gives your opponent the mental edge. Learn to burn a quiet fire within, while keeping your mind on your overall game plan. Dissimulation is a better strategy than wearing your thoughts and emotions on your sleeve.

Focus

Focus is the capacity to concentrate attention on the task at hand. Once attention is focused, there is the ability to stay focused, steering clear of potential distractions. To reach your mental potential, you need to have and maintain focus.

When in a match, you need to concentrate on many interrelated things: your overall game plan, how you are faring in the match, which serves and shots are scoring, how you feel, and so forth. After each point you store another piece of data in your mind and quickly reevaluate all these matters.

At some time during a match, what you have stored upstairs may force you to change certain aspects of your plan, maybe even your overall plan. For instance, if a particular serve has proven unsuccessful, at some point you must stop using it. If your plan to play a particular looper aggressively is failing, you must be able to switch to a less aggressive strategy. This requires an astute awareness of your present situation, an intense focus on the "now" as it relates to what you have planned. To do this successfully, you must keep everything else out of your mind.

As an athlete, you have a great amount of control over your athletic fate. The less that external factors control your table-tennis play, the more control you will have over your destiny. Improved focus at and away from the table is the main element in gaining this control and the best way to keep from being overcome by distractions.

When competing, there are several levels of focus. First, there is a single-minded commitment toward your overall goal—say, winning the "open" division. This helps you to sketch an overall plan to achieve this end, a plan that trickles into all elements of play. Next, there is a commitment toward winning your first match and each subsequent one. To focus on opponents you must devise a plan for them (one at a time) and concentrate on properly executing this plan. Last, there is a commitment toward winning each point in every match.

More than this, there is another level of focus for those desiring to rise among even the elite: a commitment to live in a way that brings about optimal play. The greatest athletes in the world constantly think about being the best, so they pattern their lives in such a way that everything they do steers them toward this end. If your goal is to be the best, you must not only play table tennis, you must *live* table tennis.

Just like all other mental facets of any sport, focus takes practice to be perfected. Rarely do novices show great concentration and focus. With experience, you will learn to vary the intensity of your focus—being able to remain committed but relaxed when not playing a match, saving your mental energy for when you need it most.

Because focus often means the difference between winning and losing at the highest level of play, how do you know if your focus is adequate? The answer lies in consistency. Your consistency against opponents at all levels is a reliable indicator. For example, do you play those rated either above you or at your level better than those beneath you? Do opponents rated 400 points beneath you on average wind up with the same number of points per game against you than those rated only 200 points beneath you? Do opponents sometimes rally from huge deficits to defeat you? Do unconventionally rubbered players always cause you problems? If you answer "yes" to any of these questions, you need to improve your focus.

One way to improve focus is by evaluating each tournament you attend, along with the training before it. Keep a booklet in which you record notes and strategies pertaining to both training and the competition. For each day of training, note the quantity and quality of sleep, what you ate, how you felt, any significant physical or mental stress during the day, training conditions, or anything that might affect your training performance. Be even more meticulous during a competition.

Keep a player profile on all opponents of any note when you compete. Write down when and where you played them, your overall strategy against them, and how you fared using this strategy. For instance, "I stayed away from my usual loop game against Alfred. I stayed up at the table, pushed, and countered. He seemed uncomfortable, ... would have been more comfortable if I pressed the attack. I won, 21 to 12, 21 to 15. Last time I played him more aggressively and won but the scores were 21 to 15, 19 to 21, 21 to 16." Record any peculiarities. "Alfred had trouble with my crosscourt nothing-ball serve. ... He has exceptionally poor footwork. ... He is a strong, aggressive blocker. When I looped fast and hard to his forehand, he would block me out of position." In such a manner you will have data that give you clues about why you performed the way you did, and this will help you learn to plot strategies and achieve success.

To become a good or even great player you must come to the table with specific playing strategies. You cannot do this unless you keep a log—assessing both your and your opponents' performance in every match you play at each tournament. In this way planning for success will become quite easy. You will seldom lose to those players you are supposed to beat and you will be surprised at how many times you will be able to defeat players rated well above you. You will attain a consistency necessary for elite play.

Performance Decline After Inactivity

All table-tennis players experience a decline in performance after a period of inactivity. Sometimes you may play a match or two, then

Figure 9.4 Jan Ove-Waldner of Sweden prepares for a forehand loop from his backhand end.

wait anywhere from a few minutes to even a few hours before another match. When playing resumes, you feel stiff and sluggish, and your motor skills are impaired. This does not last long, however, and after a handful or more of "rusty" rallies, you seem to be back where you left off.

The decline in performance is not so inevitable, however. After a period of rest, any type of warming up usually lessens the performance decline, some better than others. Not surprisingly, what makes some forms of warming up better than others is the *relevance* of the type of warm-up activity. In other words, those warm-up activities that most closely resemble actual play are best for preparing you to play again and diminishing performance decline.

In short, the most effective remedy for performance decline after resting is a warm-up that focuses on game-relevant movements. Before you even get to the table after not having played for a while, practice imagery techniques, do some stretching, and perhaps some light running in place. Next and most importantly, practice shadow stroking, footwork, and game-situation volleys away from the table— first slowly, then vigorously. (You may wish to review the section on warming up in chapter five.) In this way, by the time you face your opponent at the table, you should be hitting crisp and smooth shots and the decline in your performance will be negligible, if not absent.

Take your between-matches warm-up seriously. Constantly getting off to a poor start against opponents in the first game of a match is a sure sign that you are not adequately warmed up. Insufficient rebound from after-match performance decline may mean the difference between starting the next match down 0 to 5 or up 4 to 1.

Key Points

1. Practice mental rehearsal for the closed skills of the sport like serving.
2. Keep arousal under control; learn to burn a quiet fire within.
3. Learn to narrow focus to the immediate present during play, shutting out all distractions.
4. Warm up between matches by shadow stroking and footwork drills.

*C*hapter *10*

Thinking Like a Winner

Sweden's Kayode Kadiri preparing to serve at the 1995 World Team Cup.

*T*he old adage rings true: To be a winner you must first think like a winner. We will discuss how to improve your thinking to improve your overall play.

POSITIVE MENTAL APPLICATIONS

In what follows we suggest ways of orienting yourself to turn positive thinking into improved play.

Goal Setting

To achieve to the best of your ability, goals are essential, and setting the right kind of goals—goals that are ambitious, meaningful, and attainable—is the first important mental skill you must acquire to be a winner.

In table tennis, goal setting is intimately connected to the competitions in which you plan to participate. Serious players choose the few important tournaments each year and establish training cycles for each, so they may perform optimally. Then they weave other, less important tournaments into each training cycle. Your challenge for each cycle is to attain a long-term goal and realize many lower-level goals along the way.

Let us illustrate by setting up a hypothetical situation for you. Assume that you wish to improve your game 200 rating points within a year so that, from a rating of 2,000, you end up playing at the 2,200 level. Beginning in January, you set one goal to be playing at the 2,100 level by a tournament at the end of May, another of playing at the 2,150 level at a contest in August, and a third of playing at the 2,200 level at a tournament by the year's end. Your long-term goal is ambitious, but not unreasonable. You must now ask yourself, "What will get me from 2,000 to 2,200 in one year?" In other words, what can you do above and beyond what you have been doing to reach the 2,000 level in order to achieve a 2,200 rating?

You decide to improve your aerobic fitness as well as your explosive strength by adding a daily early morning five-mile run and some weight lifting to your weekly schedule. You also decide to receive personal instruction by a professional coach and attend a clinic in June and another in August. Last, you plan the practice drills you will be doing for your January-to-May cycle, modifying and adding to what you had been doing. The point is that you establish a difficult but reasonable long-term goal (2,200 rating), then work out a means (that is, you set up certain lower- level goals) by which you can achieve this long-term goal.

In this hypothetical situation, the yardstick of your overall success is your performance at the three major contests you plan to attend during the year: the one in May, the one in August, and the last in December. At the short-term or local level, set up monthly subgoals to help you successfully reach the goals for each of your three tournaments. Then establish weekly goals to get you where you want to be at the end of each month. Last, daily goals will add variety and intensity to your individual workouts.

At the end of each day, check your progress toward these various goals by evaluating the day's activities (training sessions, nutritional intake, sleep quality from the previous night, conditioning, etc.). The daily feedback will usually suggest *slight* modifications in your daily and weekly goals and routines, but these modifications are necessary to keep you on track for your overall goal. All this may sound excessively complicated, but it is necessary if you wish to be an elite player. Great athletes leave little to chance. Success doesn't just happen; it is well planned for and planned for well in advance.

The Right Mental Outlook

Having met the challenge of goal setting, let us turn our attention toward mental outlook. By having the right mental outlook—that is, putting the right thoughts in your head—your table-tennis performance is bound to improve. What is the best way, the most efficient way, to ensure your right thinking will lead to successful table-tennis play? In other words, what are the right thoughts to put in your head?

As an aspiring table-tennis player, as we have been emphasizing all along, most of what you do is in your hands. Train yourself to think (and really believe) that by accepting the responsibility for your destiny, you control your destiny. Your success (or failure) is less a matter of "good genes" or fate and more a matter of the amount and quality of time you put into the sport. The greatest athletes of any sport know just why they reached the top: They worked hard and intelligently.

All this is not to downplay the relevance of external factors in the overall picture of your table-tennis performance. By having a strong work ethic and believing in yourself, often you can manipulate external factors or, at least, use unfavorable conditions to your advantage. For instance, poor tournament conditions, like a slippery floor, affect every player, not just you. While other players constantly carp about this distraction and fill their head with one more reason why they cannot win, do what you can to take control of the environment. Put a wet rag near your end of the table and periodically dampen the bottoms of your shoes for better traction. If your

Figure 10.1 The 1995 World Champion, Kong Linghui of China, goes for a winner with exceptional ball placement.

opponent does not do the same, other things being equal, the advantage is yours. Your focus, consequently, will be on winning the point, not on keeping your footing.

Peak Performance

Performance at the elite rank of table tennis is more than just knowing you can play to a certain level. At the elite rank, often what it takes to win is execution *beyond* your expectations, or peak performance.

Because peak performance in table tennis takes you beyond your expectations—to personal bests and competitive victories—it uses your abilities to the fullest. Mentally, peak performance is linked with a complete and narrowed focus, an immersion in the present, a sense that your actions are effortless and automatic, and feelings of confidence, control, fearlessness, enjoyment, and relaxation. When you believe that your competence is equal to or greater than a particular task, you will persist until you are either successful or proven wrong.

How you think is related to peak performance. Athletes with high self-confidence experience peak performance more often than those with low confidence. Also, those who believe that their overall destiny is linked to their effort experience peak performance more than those who do not.

Yet, given the almost complete immersion into the present and the loss of self that accompanies peak performance, paradoxically, excellence may be harder to achieve when one is focused on trying to achieve it. If you wish to be at your best as often as possible, focus on being focused, not on winning or peer approval.

Innovation

Successful athletes differ mentally from other athletes. Overall, they are more vigorous and less tense, concern themselves less about losing, think and feel positive, and worry less about mistakes and peer evaluation.

Superior athletes are also more innovative. Though you can certainly become a very good table-tennis player without being innovative, it is doubtful that you can be the best or even reach the upper limits of your potential without innovation playing some role.

A fine example of innovation in our own sport is the Seemiller grip (see chapter one) devised by Danny and the manner of play devised to accommodate it. Danny initially adopted the grip because of a lack of proper coaching as a beginner, as well as an inability to get comfortable with the orthodox shakehands grip. However, as his love for the game grew, he found other reasons for staying with this unusual grip, not all of which were reasonable. One motive was pure stubbornness. Players and coaches told Danny that he would never get anywhere with this awkward grip, and a strong desire to prove them wrong made him persist with it. In addition, the uniqueness of the grip appealed to him. By using it, opponents would have to adjust to his style of play. Being able to switch from antispin to a spin rubber on either the forehand or the backhand during a point put an element of strategy into the game that would not have been there had he adopted the shakehands style. Last, and perhaps most important, Danny had international goals and decided that the uniqueness of his grip would help him to compete more effectively against the highly talented Europeans and Asians. At his best, Danny was rated 19th in the world. This is not bad for one who did not have regular access to the finest players in the world during his prime.

We are not suggesting that to be an elite table-tennis player you must take innovation to the extreme that Danny did. Nevertheless it should be a part of a well constructed program for success. Versatility is a must for serious competition and innovation is one way to be versatile. Constantly experiment with new service techniques. Against problematic serves, think up new ways of returning them consistent with your style of play. Overall, be innovative in developing strategies against players or styles of play that trouble you. Learn from other players as well, both the great ones and the not-so-great, and apply their ideas and techniques to your playing.

Key Points

1. Set reasonable long-term and short-term goals.
2. Take responsibility for your achievements by learning to view success and failure as a matter of your preparation and efforts.
3. Strive for and expect peak performance at important competitions if you have trained well.
4. Be creative in your mental approach to the game.

OVERCOMING OBSTACLES

To constantly improve, top-notch athletes must fight through slumps and plateaus, and overcome the mental stress associated with them. Those that make it to the top—just like the majority who never do—experience anxiety, worry, and failure at each step of the way. Persistence and a hopeful outlook are essential but, in addition to this, athletes must continually develop new and better preparation and fitness strategies to get them beyond the hurdles they face along the way. In this final section, we show how thinking like a winner may enable you to overcome or avoid performance obstacles.

Slumpbusting

A slump is a decline in performance that, because of its length, cannot be explained by normal cyclic variations. As most successful athletes know, slumps happen to everyone and slumps eventually pass.

To overcome a slump, first, you must have some measure of your baseline performance before the slump. This is the most crucial piece of information for, without this, you have no means of identifying a slump. Second, you must know how much and how long your play has declined. Only by measuring the severity of your slump can you plan for an effective remedy. Third, you must look into the possible causes of your slump. Assuming that the first two aspects are unproblematic, we discuss the last of these bits of information only.

The causes of slumps are varied. A slump may have a physical cause such as injury, illness, fatigue, or poor eating. The cause may be mental, like a failed relationship, depression, or even lack of focus. Technical reasons are often factors. Perhaps you have slightly, though unknowingly, modified the follow-through of your forehand counterdrive so you have inconsistent ball placement. Last, equipment problems may be responsible. For instance, playing with old rubber or shoes that give you unsure footing may lead to a slump. Of course, any combination of these factors may be at play too.

Once you have identified a slump, draw up a thorough list of the possible causes. Next, investigate these and dismiss those that are irrelevant or improbable. From the candidates that remain, investigate each further in a logical and structured fashion. From these, dismiss those that cannot be relevant. The remaining candidates, if the initial pool was complete, are likely relevant causes. In such a way it is possible to identify the causes of your slump.

Once you have pinpointed the relevant causes, begin a plan of action with specific remedial goals. First, if the cause of the slump is persistent, then establish a goal to get rid of the cause. If you have fallen back on some mechanically unsound stroking habits, plan how you will unlearn these habits. If your poorer play is caused by putting on 10 pounds of body fat, design a course of action to lose this extra weight.

Next, set an overall performance goal. If, for instance, you were playing at the 1,700 level before a slump took you down to 1,550, then you or your coach must decide whether a sub-1,700 goal, a super-1,700 goal, or a return to your previous level of performance is reasonable. This depends on the nature of the cause and the severity of the slump.

With an overall performance goal established, set daily training goals to assist in getting to your performance goal and eliminating the effects of the cause.

As always, after analyzing the slump, be patient. It takes time for slumps to pass, so do not expect your remedial efforts to be immediately effective. It may even be wise to take time off. In most cases of slumping, there is a strong negative emotional strain that you need to break before you can overcome the slump, and time away lets you heal emotionally.

Time away from the game can also help your analysis of the causes of the slump. Because your analysis occurs outside the training environment, it is generally more objective and positive. If you decide to take time off, the length of the time off should be proportional to the severity of your slump. If the slump is slight, then a couple of days is usually sufficient. If the slump is severe, then you may need a week or two away from play.

During a lengthy respite, if the cause of the slump is not overtraining, you may do some conditioning such as running or weight lifting, but avoid anything *specifically* associated with table tennis. You may be uncomfortable with taking more than a couple days off from play, but this is not unusual. However, if your goal is to get out of your slump as quickly as possible and if time away from table tennis will ultimately help to bring this about, then take the necessary time off.

Key Points

1. Know your prior performance baseline.
2. Measure the length of slump.
3. Examine all possible causes.
4. Set an overall performance goal to get rid of the slump.
5. Be patient with the results, especially if the slump has been lengthy.

Overtraining

There is a false bias among serious athletes of all sports that to get better you must constantly train more and harder. In addition, this bias infects other aspects of performance. Players tend to attribute any leveling off or diminution in performance to lack of intensity or practice time.

On one hand, this thinking is not completely foolhardy. For continual improvement you need extraordinary training intensity and many training hours. Nevertheless, too much intensity and time can

Figure 10.2 Kong Linghui demonstrates perfect form for the forehand counterdrive.

sometimes be the very thing that causes a decline in performance. Sometimes table-tennis players fail to improve, not because they do too little, but because they do too much. They overtrain.

Overtraining is a condition in which mental or physical stress overwhelms you, and your table-tennis play levels off or declines.

What is unusual about overtraining, however, is that it is generally the last thing you look for when you are playing subpar. More often than not, when performance is off, you will change your practice drills, playing strategies, eating behavior, playing clothes, and even your lucky charm before you will consider that you might have been doing too much.

How, then, do you know when you have been overtraining? Overtraining is recognizable by many symptoms: being easily fatigued, always feeling overtired, an unusually low or high resting pulse, an increase in diastolic blood pressure, reduced appetite, weight loss, long and frequent sleep, headaches, reduced reaction time, and poor performance of skilled movements. Smart players, as we emphasize throughout, monitor all aspects of their training behavior—even their physical and mental well-being. You must learn to do the same if you wish to have constantly intense workouts and steady improvement in your play.

The symptoms of overtraining suggest checks. First, constantly monitor your waking heart rate by checking your early morning pulse. If it is elevated by eight beats per minute more than the previous week, you are probably overtraining. Second, monitor your waking body weight. If it is down by three pounds or more on any day, then you are likely to be overtraining. Third, note any problems with your sleep. Insomnia of any sort is often a sign of overtraining.

Learn your training limits, then plan your daily workouts by carefully writing what you will do each week before you do it. In this manner, you intelligently vary the length, intensity, and type of your daily workouts.

Key Point

1. Carefully monitor all aspects of your training to guard against overtraining.

Maladaptive Behavior

Though this may seem puzzling, maladaptive athletic behavior thrives at all levels of sport, including the elite level. In this section we focus on two maladaptive behaviors that are mentally linked with slumps and plateaus: learned helplessness and anxiety.

Learned Helplessness. Just as continued success brings about further success, continued failure creates a mental atmosphere in which failure is expected and usually occurs. Some unsuccessful athletes, through improper coaching or advice, have been conditioned to fail; others, by themselves, have adopted maladaptive mental attitudes and literally have taught themselves to fail. All routinely unsuccessful athletes, however, feel as if success and failure are entirely out of their control. This phenomenon is referred to as "learned helplessness."

Through regular exposure to failure, you begin to perceive that successful outcomes are impossible and you come to expect that winning is outside your control. This, in turn, produces behavior that makes future success impossible.

Helpless athletes assess their level of competence as low. They perceive they have a low ability to change factors that contribute to unsuccessful performance. More than this, they need not even perform poorly to have this perception. Sometimes even flawless performance may bring about thoughts of incompetence and failure. Moreover, they fail to use new competition strategies when old ones are unsuccessful or fail to develop any strategies at all.

Motivationally, helpless athletes show little persistence toward obstacles or tend to avoid them altogether. Emotionally, only success produces feelings of pride and satisfaction, whereas failure brings about little pride and satisfaction, regardless of the effort.

Because all athletes at some time experience some degree of helplessness, to reach the height of your talent, develop strategies to prevent or overcome helplessness. First, whether in practice or in competition, learn to focus on effort rather than outcome. Daily goal setting, charting, and audiovisual feedback may help. Also, an improved focus toward both task-relevant information and task-relevant preparation strategies will help to finely tune table-tennis-specific skills. Second, in the analysis of your performance decline, learn to separate relevant and important causes from irrelevant and unimportant ones. Helpless athletes exaggerate the causal strength of factors that have only a slight influence on their performance and are completely beyond their control. Focus only on relevant factors and those that you can control. Last, learn coping skills. We discuss some in the following section dealing with anxiety.

Anxiety. Anxiety is perhaps the most common type of maladaptive behavior, a problem all athletes have to deal with at some time. Historically, anxiety has been viewed as something that only impairs performance. Recent findings indicate, however, that anxiety both improves and impairs performance, depending on athletes' expectations regarding their ability to cope with it. Nevertheless, if you have experienced or are experiencing debilitating anxiety, then some mental readjustment is probably necessary. Let us now turn to specific coping strategies for debilitating anxiety.

One such coping strategy is massage. Massage before or after exercise may significantly decrease tension, depression, anger, confusion, and fatigue. Because of this, massage may help you physically and mentally prepare for a competition.

Progressive relaxation is another coping tool. Progressive relaxation increases your ability to handle stress and effectively lowers arousal. You begin with a slow and deep breath. Feel the stress of the air within, then concentrate on lessening the stress as you exhale. Then, starting with the dominant arm, slowly and deliberately tense and relax its muscles. Work the other arm next, then the face, neck, shoulders, back, stomach, buttocks, legs (one at a time), and feet. With each contraction, focus on the feeling of increased tension. When relaxing, focus on the feeling of released tension. If you find it beneficial, practice progressive relaxation daily and before important matches during tournaments.

Hypnosis is a third commonly used coping skill. However, the effects of hypnosis are dubious. David Onestak relates that hypnosis without motivational suggestion does not lead to superior performance and that motivational instructions are equally effective when given in either the hypnotic or the waking state. This implies it is the motivational instruction given during hypnosis and not hypnosis itself that is responsible for clearing away debilitating anxiety. Consequently, if you have made good use of hypnosis in the past, an equally effective and less costly alternative may be motivational instruction.

Key Points

1. Focus on effort, not outcome.
2. Separate relevant and important causes of maladaptive behavior from those that are irrelevant and unimportant.
3. If necessary, learn and use coping strategies.

To be a winner, it is important to think like a winner. First, learn to set reasonable long-term goals and develop short-term goals and strategies to reach these. Second, narrow your focus to the immediate present, and maintain a general disregard for the outcome. Third, develop confidence-building techniques along with a coach or training partner. Fourth, through innovation and planned variation in your practice sessions, train in such a manner that you reduce the likelihood of performance impairment and plateaus.

Appendix

Training Schedule and Cycle for Professional Players

7:15 a.m.	Wake and eat meal one—25 grams protein, 100 grams carbohydrate
8:45 a.m.	Light carbohydrate preworkout meal (meal two)—50 grams
9:30 a.m.-12:00 noon	Morning practice session
12:15 p.m.	Meal three—25 grams protein, 100 grams carbohydrate
12:30-2:00 p.m.	Afternoon nap or rest
2:15 p.m.	Light carbohydrate preworkout meal (meal four)—50 grams
3:00-5:00 p.m.	Afternoon practice session
5:15 p.m.	Meal five—25 grams protein, 100 grams carbohydrate
7:30-8:30 p.m.	Evening practice session
8:45 p.m.	Meal six—25 grams protein, 100 grams carbohydrate
2:00 a.m.	Meal seven—25 grams protein, 100 grams carbohydrate

Table A.1 Sample Cycle for Professional Player

Generalized conditioning phase

	M	T	W	TH	F	S
Morning session	Stroking Footwork	8 mile run Stroking Footwork	Stroking Footwork	8 mile run Stroking Footwork	Stroking Footwork	8 mile run Stroking Footwork
Afternoon session	Lifting	Stroking Footwork	Lifting	Stroking Footwork	Lifting	Stroking Footwork
Evening session	Service Return	Service Return	Service Return	Service Return	Service Return	Service Return

Specialized conditioning phase

	M	T	W	TH	F	S
Morning session	Lifting Stroking Footwork	8 mile run Stroking Footwork	Stroking Footwork	Lifting Stroking Footwork	8 mile run Stroking Footwork	Match play
Afternoon session	Service Return Game situation	Service Return Game situation	Service Return Game situation	Service Return Game situation	Service Return Game situation	Service Return Game situation
Evening session	Problem areas	Problem areas	Problem areas	Problem areas	Problem areas	Problem areas

Precompetitive phase

	M	T	W	TH	F	S
Morning session	Lifting Stroking Footwork	Stroking Footwork	8 mile run Stroking Footwork	Stroking Footwork	Stroking Footwork	Stroking Footwork
Afternoon session	Service Return Game situation	Match play	Service Return Game situation	Match play	Service Return Game situation	Match play
Evening session	Problem areas	Problem areas	Problem areas	Problem areas	Problem areas	Problem areas

Index

A bout the Authors

Dan Seemiller knows table tennis, drawing from years of professional competition, international-level coaching, and his love of the game.

Seemiller was the #1 player on the U.S. table tennis team from 1973 to 1983. He was U.S. singles champion 5 times and doubles champion 11 times, winning 8 years in a row. In 1977 he and his doubles partner made the quarter finals of the World Championships—the first U.S. team to go that far in international competition. During his playing career, Seemiller reached a world ranking of #19.

Seemiller, who coached the U.S. National Men's table tennis team in 1988 and 1989, has been teaching table tennis at clinics and camps for more than 20 years. He is the inventor of the American "Seemiller grip," which combines two other popular grips to provide better racquet control.

Past-president of the United States Table Tennis Association (USTTA) from 1990 to 1995, Seemiller was unanimously inducted into the USTTA Hall of Fame in 1995. He now coaches and travels throughout the world, giving clinics on table tennis and producing instructional videos. For more information on Seemiller's clinics and videos, write Dan at P.O. Box 608, New Carlisle, Indiana 46552.

Seemiller lives with his wife, Valerie, and their children, Sara and Daniel, Jr. He enjoys golf, softball, and yard work.

Coauthor **Mark Holowchak** combines a keen interest in sport performance with a great enthusiasm for table tennis. He has been an avid player since 1973 and has been coaching power lifters at the University of Pittsburgh since 1988.

Holowchak has written numerous articles on fitness, nutrition, strength training, philosophy, and sport psychology for weightlifting and table tennis magazines. He has a master's degree in philosophy from Wayne State University in Detroit and a master's degree in history and philosophy of science from the University of Pittsburgh. A member of the USTTA, he is completing his PhD in history and philosophy of science at the University of Pittsburgh.

Holowchak lives in Pittsburgh, Pennsylvania, and enjoys lifting weights, reading, and traveling.

Additional HK Resources

Larry Hodges

in cooperation with United States Table Tennis Association

1993 • Paper • 160 pp
Item PHOD0403
ISBN 0-87322-403-5
$14.95 ($21.95 Canadian)

Robert M. Nideffer, PhD

1992 • Paper • 152 pp
Item PNID0463
ISBN 0-88011-463-0
$12.95 ($17.95 Canadian)

Michael J. Alter

1990 • Paper • 168 pp
Item PALT0381
ISBN 0-88011-381-2
$15.95 ($23.95 Canadian)

If you'd like to request a **FREE** copy of our Sports & Coaching catalog, which features listings and descriptions of sport-specific and coaching resources on a wide range of subject areas, call **TOLL-FREE**
1-800-747-4457

Human Kinetics
The Premier Publisher for Sports & Fitness
http://www.humankinetics.com/
2335

To request more information or to place your order, U.S. customers call
TOLL-FREE 1-800-747-4457.
Customers outside the U.S. use appropriate telephone number/address shown in the front of this book.

Prices subject to change.